Boats on the River Douro

Porto is actually the oldest city in Portugal, a country which took its name from the tiny city-state from which Portugal eventually emerged. There's an old Portuguese saying that Porto works while Lisbon plays and, indeed, the city has always been the centre of Portugal's industry. It was here that the ships were built for Portugal's famous navigators who helped open up a maritime empire stretching from Brazil to Macau. However, its most famous industry has long been port wine, a name given by the city but whose production is largely based on the south banks of the River Douro in Vila Nova de Gaia. Technically a separate city, it is closely linked to Porto by a series of impressive bridges and no trip to Porto is complete without a visit to its famous port wine lodges, whose neon signs light up the skyline after dark.

If you're fit enough to negotiate its hills, Porto is a great place to explore on foot: beyond the riverfront lies a fascinating city of broad squares, Neoclassical buildings and Baroque churches, many of them lavishly decorated with *azulejos*, the beautiful glazed ceramic tiles which also embellish many houses and public buildings. It's easy to get around on public transport, too, with a modern and efficient metro system and a good network of buses. There are also three vintage tram routes, one wending its way along the riverfront to Porto's upmarket seaside suburb of Foz do Douro, whose sands face the roaring waves of the Atlantic.

Porto also boasts some excellent museums, including the Museu Nacional Soares dos Reis with its amazing collection of art from Portugal and its former colonies, and the Fundação Serralves, featuring contemporary art in beautifully landscaped grounds.

When to visit

Porto's summers are hot with average daytime temperatures of around 26°C in July and August. Better times to visit are September and October which are a more comfortable 21–23°C, as is June, when you can enjoy the city's main festival, the Festa de São João. However, it's rarely cold in Porto even in midwinter, when it can even feel warm when the sun appears. Be aware, however, that Porto's climate is heavily influenced by the Atlantic and it can rain with a vengeance: the wettest months tend to be October to January.

The city centre suffered a dramatic loss of population between 1970 and 2010, when tourism started to inject new life. Now, many of the previously abandoned or run-down mansions and shops have been given a new lease of life and have become chic hotels and fashionable restaurants or cafés. Traditional gems remain, too, including the famous Livraria Lello bookshop, allegedly the inspiration for J K Rowling's *Harry Potter* stories.

If you want a break from the city, there are easy escapes out to the sea at Foz do Douro and neighbouring Matosinhos, famed for its fish restaurants, while the metro can whisk you up to Vila do Conde, a historic town with a fabulous Atlantic beach. Alternatively, get a taste of the beautiful interior in Amarante, a quaint town sitting on a tributary of the River Douro, just an hour's bus ride from the city.

What's in a name?

O Porto means 'the port' in Portuguese, but you'll often see the city referred to as **Oporto** in English – probably because of a misconception. In Portuguese, the article "o" (meaning the) is often used as in the sentence "a familia mudou-se para o Porto" (the family moved to Porto). O Porto was probably heard as one word, hence Oporto. Of course the same confusion does not apply to the drink port, which is as associated with a particular place as much as champagne or Madeira, and in fact, Porto has given its name to the country itself: originally named Portus Cale by the Romans, the area around Porto was the first to become the independent country which became known as Portugal.

Festa de São João

Where to...

SHOP

There are plenty of out-of-town mega shopping malls, but the city centre is made up of an appealing mixture of lovely traditional tile-fronted grocery stores, quirky local stores and chic boutiques. The long, pedestrianized Rua da Santa Catarina, near the wonderful Bolhão food market, is the place for everyday clothes shopping, while the area around Praça da Lisboa is where you'll find designer and vintage shops. It's worth also heading to Rua das Flores, near São Bento, which is also good for chic, independent outlets.

OUR FAVOURITES: Armazén p.78. **Arcádia** p.54. **Fernandes Mattos & Co** p.54.

EAT

Porto's cuisine is typical of northern Portugal. Grilled meat – including game and the local speciality, tripe –feature prominently on menus, as does *bacalhau* (dried salted cod). You'll probably find all of this at either the simple restaurants dotted round the city, or in the chic pricier restaurants near the riverside. Don't miss Portugal's famous pastries, either, including the ever-popular *pastéis de nata*.

OUR FAVOURITES: The Yeatman p.70. **Cantinho do Avillez** p.57. **Piolho d'Ouro** p.58.

DRINK

Porto is forever associated with port and there are endless possibilities to try it at tasting rooms, restaurants and port wine lodges. There are plenty of other tipples to savour, too, with Portugal's non-fortified wines being of excellent quality. Superbock beer is fairly ubiquitous and there's a growing trend for local craft beers in the city, too. Local brandies are worth sampling, and you should definitely try a caipirinha, a potent Brazilian cocktail made from a rather drinkable mix of distilled sugar cane, cachaça and lime juice.

OUR FAVOURITES: Café Candelabro p.55. **BASE** p.58. **Praia dos Ingleses** p.99.

GO OUT

Porto has a thriving nightlife scene, though note that most clubs don't get going much before midnight. There's a good concentration of fashionable clubs and bars along Rua Galeria de Paris and Rua Cândido dos Reis off Praça de Lisboa, while the streets around the pedestrianized Travessa de Cedofeita have some of the best alternative bars, many which have nights featuring guest DJs.

OUR FAVOURITES: O Meu Mercedes é Maior que o Teu p.35. **Plano B** p.59. **Casa da Ló** p.58.

Porto at a glance

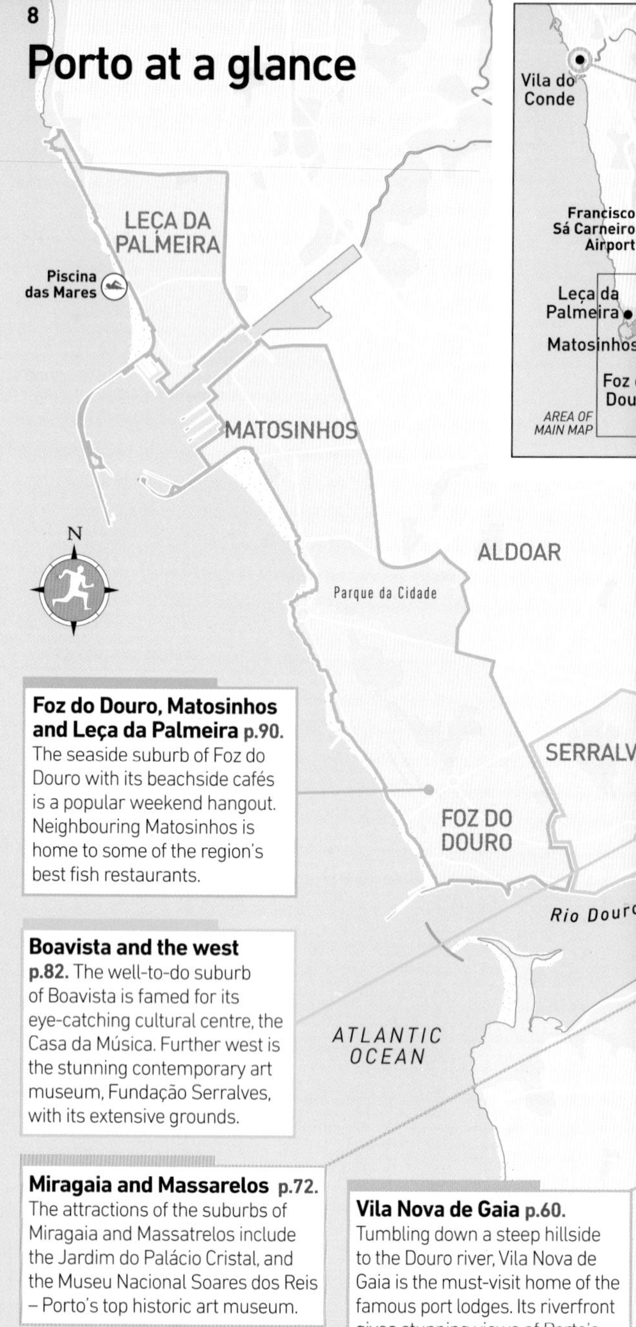

Foz do Douro, Matosinhos and Leça da Palmeira **p.90.** The seaside suburb of Foz do Douro with its beachside cafés is a popular weekend hangout. Neighbouring Matosinhos is home to some of the region's best fish restaurants.

Boavista and the west **p.82.** The well-to-do suburb of Boavista is famed for its eye-catching cultural centre, the Casa da Música. Further west is the stunning contemporary art museum, Fundação Serralves, with its extensive grounds.

Miragaia and Massarelos **p.72.** The attractions of the suburbs of Miragaia and Massatrelos include the Jardim do Palácio Cristal, and the Museu Nacional Soares dos Reis – Porto's top historic art museum.

Vila Nova de Gaia **p.60.** Tumbling down a steep hillside to the Douro river, Vila Nova de Gaia is the must-visit home of the famous port lodges. Its riverfront gives stunning views of Porto's historic core opposite.

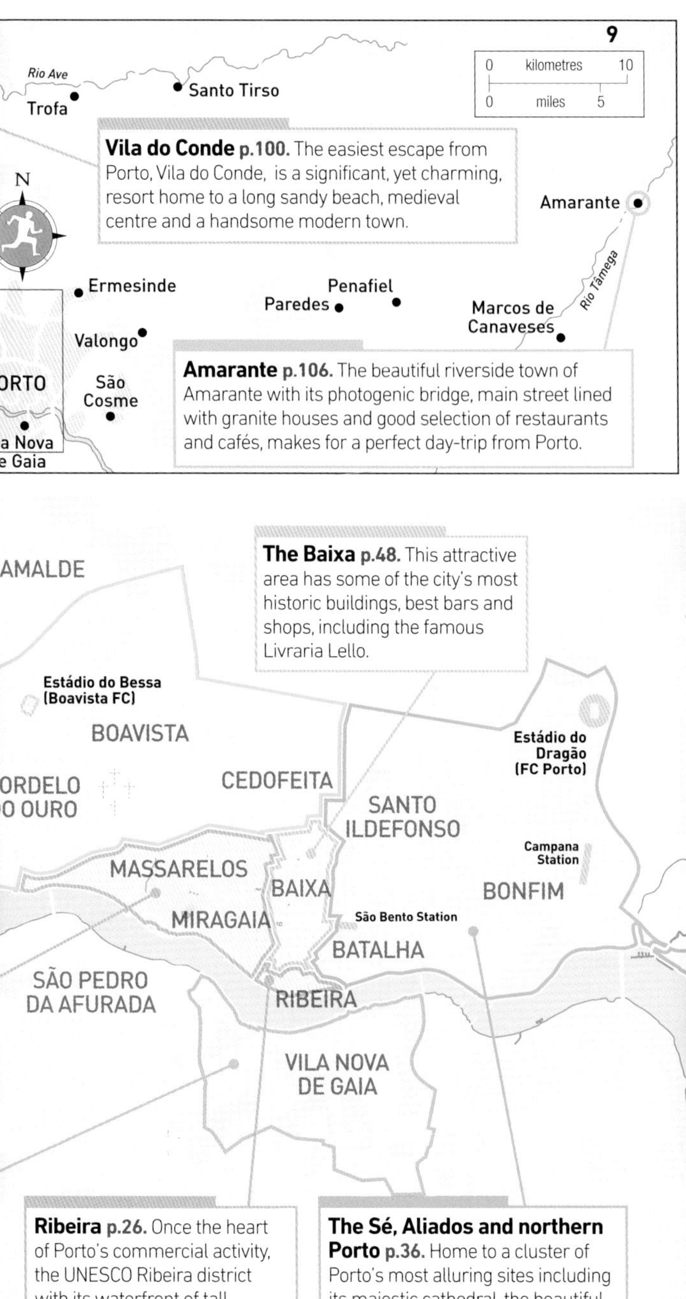

Rio Ave
Trofa
Santo Tirso
0 kilometres 10
0 miles 5
Vila do Conde p.100. The easiest escape from Porto, Vila do Conde, is a significant, yet charming, resort home to a long sandy beach, medieval centre and a handsome modern town.
N
Amarante
Rio Tâmega
Ermesinde
Penafiel
Paredes
Marcos de Canaveses
Valongo
ORTO
São Cosme
a Nova e Gaia
Amarante p.106. The beautiful riverside town of Amarante with its photogenic bridge, main street lined with granite houses and good selection of restaurants and cafés, makes for a perfect day-trip from Porto.
AMALDE
The Baixa p.48. This attractive area has some of the city's most historic buildings, best bars and shops, including the famous Livraria Lello.
Estádio do Bessa (Boavista FC)
BOAVISTA
Estádio do Dragão (FC Porto)
ORDELO O OURO
CEDOFEITA
SANTO ILDEFONSO
Campana Station
MASSARELOS
BAIXA
BONFIM
MIRAGAIA
São Bento Station
BATALHA
SÃO PEDRO DA AFURADA
RIBEIRA
VILA NOVA DE GAIA
Ribeira p.26. Once the heart of Porto's commercial activity, the UNESCO Ribeira district with its waterfront of tall, colourful medieval houses is understandably one of the most popular destinations in the city.
The Sé, Aliados and northern Porto p.36. Home to a cluster of Porto's most alluring sites including its majestic cathedral, the beautiful São Bento station and the Bolhão market. Further north lies the famous Estádio do Dragão.

17 Things not to miss

It's not possible to see everything that Porto has to offer in one trip – and we don't suggest you try. What follows is a selective taste of Porto's highlights, from the city's famous port wine lodges to its coolest night spots.

∨ PORT WINE LODGES

p.64

Take a tour and sample the delicious port at Vila Nova de Gaia's historic wine lodges, some of which date back hundreds of years.

∧ A DRINK AT RIBEIRA

p.26

Watch the comings and goings with a glass of white port from the picturesque Douro riverside district of Ribeira, the city's ancient docks.

> PALÁCIO DA BOLSA

p.31

The wealth of Porto's nineteenth-century traders is demonstrated by the opulence of the former stock exchange, built in the style of a Neoclassical palace.

< PONTE DE DOM LUÍS I

p.27 & p.40

You can walk over the top or bottom tier of this historic bridge. Built by a colleague of Gustav Eiffel, it offers superb views over the Douro.

∧ TORRE DOS CLÉRIGOS

p.50

Admire the cityscape from this 75m-high historic tower, designed by famous Italian architect Nicolau Nasoni in the 1760s.

< A NIGHT OUT IN THE BAIXA

p.58

Head down Travessa do Cedofeita or Rua Cândido dos Reis for the liveliest bar and club crawl, though don't expect much action before midnight.

> THE SÉ

p.36

Dating back to the twelfth century, Porto's oldest building has magnificent cloisters and also boasts the city's top views from its terrace.

13

∨ SÃO BENTO

p.42

You don't have to take a train to admire the stunning tiled interior of the city station, decorated with around 20,000 glazed tiles.

∧ TRAM TO FOZ DO DOURO

p.90

Hop on the vintage tram out to Porto's alluring seaside suburb of Foz do Douro, the route hugging the banks of the Douro River.

< LIVRARIA LELLO

p.52

Check out the decor of this amazing bookshop, whose lavish Art Nouveau interior is said to have inspired the *Harry Potter* stories.

> JARDIM DO PALÁCIO DE CRISTAL

p.76

Chill out at the city centre's main park, where a series of terraces and lawns provide dazzling views over the Douro.

< FC PORTO

p.43

Catch a match at the famous Estádio do Dragão, home to FC Porto, the former European Champions who launched the career of José Mourinho.

∨ BOAT TRIP

p.127

Take a boat ride under Porto's six impressive bridges that connect the steep banks of the Douro, each one a remarkable feat of engineering.

∧ CAFÉ MAJESTIC

p.45

Have a coffee, cake or even a full meal at the city's most ornate *belle époque* café, a riot of mirrors and celestial cherubs.

> MATOSINHOS

p.95

Join Porto locals on their Sunday lunchtime pilgrimage to the good-value fish restaurants in the earthy seaside town of Matosinhos, with its decent sandy beaches.

< CASA DA MÚSICA

p.86

Catch a concert at architect Rem Koolhaas' cultural centre, an ultra modern delight which has revitalized the Boavista district.

∨ FUNDAÇÃO SERRALVES

p.87

Visit this stunning contemporary art museum, designed by renowned Portuguese architect Álvaro Siza Vieira and set in beautiful parkland.

Day one in Porto

Sé p.36. Admire Porto's oldest building, then get your bearings from the broad terrace out front.

Walk through Barredo p.28. Head downhill through the maze-like steps and alleys of the Barredo district.

Ribeira p.26. Explore Porto's riverfont, once rough and ready but now the city's tourist hub.

Funicular dos Guindais p.28. Take this fun modern funicular which whisks you back up to the level of the main city.

Lunch p.45. Seek out *Casa Guedes* for its legendary pork sandwiches and outdoor tables facing a pretty square.

Ponte de Dom Luís I p.40. Make your way over the top tier of the Ponte de Dom Luís bridge for fantastic views over the river.

Teleférico de Gaia p.61. You can walk down to Vila Nova de Gaia, but is more fun to take the cable car which gently glides down to the riverside.

Port wine lodges p.64. Take a leisurely tour of one of Porto's famous port wine lodges, which include the chance to sample a glass, or three, at the end.

Dinner p.32. Walk back over the bridge to Ribeira. Here you'll find *Adega de São Nicolãu*, an excellent spot for meat, game or fish.

Drink p.55. *Café Candelabro* is a great chillout spot, with a range of drinks in a former bookshop.

Sé

Walk through Barredo

Teleférico de Gaia

Day two

Palácio da Bolsa p.31. Check out the riches that Portugal's merchants once brought to the city at the wonderfully ornate former stock exchange.

Igreja de São Francisco p.30. Porto's most fabulous church, a dazzling assembly of gilded carvings contrasting with the eerie catacombs full of scrubbed bones.

Tram ride p.75. Hop on one of Porto's vintage trams. The circular route #22 takes you around the city centre.

Lunch p.57. There are excellent steaks, *francesinhos* and *petiscos* at the modern *Cervejaria Brasão*.

Torre dos Clérigos p.50. Designed by Italian architect Nicolau Nasoni, the top of this distinctive tower gives amazing views across the city.

Livraria Lello p.52. You don't have to be a *Harry Potter* fan to appreciate the stunning interior, and exterior, of this historic bookshop, which was the former haunt of JK Rowling.

Fundação Serralves p.87. Take the bus to Porto's top cultural attraction, with changing exhibitions in a sumptuous building set in impressive grounds.

Dinner p.57. Sample affordable food from one of the country's top chefs at *Cantinho do Avillez*.

Drink p.58. Chill out at *Casa da Ló*, a former bakery, now a hip spot with a small garden.

Torre dos Clérigos

Livraria Lello

Fundação Serralves

Shopping

There's a wide selection of charming traditional shops, though chic boutiques and mega shopping malls will also keep serious shoppers happy.

Breakfast p.45. Start the day in the city's famous and ornate *Café Majestic*, before the crowds take over.

A Pérola do Bolhão p.44. Opposite Porto's fabulous Bolhão market, this grocery store has barely changed since it opened in 1917 – it's a great place to stock up.

Livraria Lello p.52. Even if you don't want to buy a book, this is a must-see magical store that inspired JK Rowlings' *Harry Potter*.

Alameda Shopping p.44. The place to go for some serious shopping, with over 120 shops and a giant hypermarket.

Lunch p.79. Have an inexpensive lunch in the Zen-like calm of *Rota do Chá*'s garden.

Rua Miguel Bombarda p.77. This long street is lined with Porto's coolest galleries and boutiques showcasing cutting-edge art, fashion and design.

Rua das Flores p.50. Browse along this fashionable pedestrianized street that's home to great chocolate shops, delis, boutiques and cafés.

Loja de Vinhos do Douro e do Porto p.32. Sample Porto's famous tipple at the Port Wine Institute's shop and showroom.

Armazén p.78. It's name means warehouse, and it's a treasure trove of bric-à-brac and curios.

Dinner p.33. Enjoy nouveau Portuguese cuisine with a river view at *Bacalhau*.

A Pérola do Bolhão

Rota do Chá'

Rua das Flores

Kid's Porto

Portugal is very child friendly and Porto has a diverse range of attractions to appeal to children of all ages, from trams to museums and beaches.

Torre dos Clérigos p.50. Challenge the kids to climb the two hundred stairs to Porto's best viewing platform at the top of a 75m tower.

Douro bridges cruise p.127. See Porto from the water on these fun fifty-minute boat trips along the Douro.

World of Discoveries p.73. This informative themed museum takes kids back to the time of Portugal's maritime explorations: there's even an indoor boat ride for them to enjoy.

Museu dos Transportes e Comunicações p.72. In the amazing former customs house building, this vast museum displays everything from vintage computers to classic cars.

Lunch p.34. Try Porto's legendary *francesinhas* at *Verso em Pedra*.

Bazar de Paris p.44. Pop into the city's oldest toyshop: it may not be huge but it certainly has some vintage gems.

Teleférico de Gaia p.61. Take the cable car from Jardim do Morro metro stop (it's a great trip from São Bento metro to get there) for a stunning ride down to Vila Nova de Gaia.

Zoo Santo Inácio p.62. A fun zoo where you can walk through a tunnel that gets you up-close to Asian lions.

Dinner p.46. You can't go wrong with chicken and chips, and *Pedro dos Frangos* specializes in it.

Douro bridges cruise

World of Discoveries

Zoo Santo Inácio

Budget Porto

Portugal is inexpensive at the best of times but you can save even more by visiting this range of attractions that are completely free to enter, or less expensive than most.

Centro Português de Fotografia **p.51.** There's free entry to this fascinating photographic museum housed in the eerie former city prison.

Jardim do Palácio de Cristal **p.76.** Chill out at these tranquil gardens whose terraces spill down towards the Douro.

Lunch **p.58.** Eat inside the cavernous *Piolho d'Ouro* for large portions of good value meals.

Cais da Ribeira **p.26.** Porto's riverfront provides constant free entertainment in the form of buskers, street artists, people-watching and river views.

Ponte de Dom Luís I **p.40.** It's a spectacular walk over the two-tiered bridge: the top tier doubles as a metro line.

Mosteiro de Serra de Pilar **p.61.** Admire the views from the terrace of this circular monastery.

Churchill's **p.65.** Take a tour of one of the least expensive port wine lodges and enjoy a free port tasting.

Sé **p.36.** Porto's ancient cathedral is free to enter, while the terrace at the front offers some of the best views over the city.

Drink **p.47.** Make your way to the *Guindalense Futebal Clube* café-bar, which has inexpensive drinks, snacks and views to die for.

Dinner **p.81.** Squeeze into the titchy *Taberna Santo António*, where you can sample bargain daily specials.

Centro Português de Fotografia

Jardim do Palácio de Cristal

Mosteiro de Serra de Pilar

A day by the sea

If you've got time and have done the big sights, take a break from the city with a day out by the sea at the well-to-do suburb of Foz do Douro or neighbouring Matosinhos.

Tram to Foz do Douro p.90. Tram #1 is a wonderful ride out to the sea, following the banks of the River Douro.

Jardim do Passeio Alegre p.90. Take a leisurely walk to the seafront via these gardens, which are fringed by towering palms.

Breakfast p.96. Head for *Tavi*, a gem of a café with a sea-facing terrace and a sumptuous array of pastries.

Foz seafront p.92. Make your way up Foz do Douro's seafront promenade, stopping off at a series of sandy beaches.

Parque da Cidade p.94. Take a stroll though Portugal's largest urban park, dotted with lakes, lawns and flowerbeds.

Lunch p.96. Hop on a bus up the coast to neighbouring Matosinhos, famed for its fish restaurants – *Dom Peixe* is always a good bet.

Matosinos market p.95. Walk up to the expansive Matosinhos market, filled with an astonishing array of fish of all sizes, as well as fruit, vegetables and flowers.

Piscina das Mares p.95. With your own transport, you can head a little north to these sleek sea pools, designed by Portugal's most famous architect.

Dinner p.98. Take the bus back to Foz do Douro for a beachside meal at *Praia da Luz* to watch the sun set.

Foz seafront

Matosinos market

Piscina das Mares

CALEM

PLACES

Douro River and Ribeira

Ribeira

Ribeira (which means riverside) is a fascinating hotch-potch of tall, colourful houses piled one behind the other on the steep slopes leading down the Douro. This was the heart of the medieval city and the hub of its commerce. With the dramatic Ponte de Dom Luís I on one side and the distinctive port wine lodges opposite, it's undeniably attractive, its riverbanks lined with cafés and restaurants that attract no shortage of tourists, buskers and street entertainers. Just back from the river, you'll find some of the city's most historic buildings, including the Casa do Infante, believed to be the former house of Henry the Navigator; the impressive fourteenth-century Igreja de São Francisco; and Porto's former stock exchange, the Bolsa, which gives an insight into the commercial riches that once poured into the city.

Cais da Ribeira

MAP p.28, POCKET MAP E8

The arcaded quayside, the **Cais da Ribeira**, is a highly picturesque run of restaurants and cafés looking across the river Douro to the port wine lodges on the other side. Lined with tall, medieval houses, this used to be the centre for Porto's trade, with *bacalhau*, cotton, wine and other goods being unloaded from the boats that plied the river Douro. Today, the pedestrianized riverfront has become the tourist heart of the city, with places to eat, buskers and hawkers. It can get crowded, but it's still an atmospheric and attractive part of the city – find a perch overlooking the river and you can easily while away an afternoon here.

Praça da Ribeira

Towards the Ponte de Dom Luís I, by the arch leading to the Ascensor da Ribeira (see p.28), a plaque known as the *Alminhas* (the souls) marks the spot where locals lost their lives fleeing Napoleon's troops in 1809. A pontoon bridge collapsed, flinging the people into the river where many drowned.

Praça da Ribeira

MAP p.28, POCKET MAP E8

Café tables spill out onto Ribeira's attractive main square, **Praça da Ribeira**, which is marked by two fountains. One fountain is a modern cube sculpture, known as Cubo da Ribeira, designed in the 1970s by artist José Rodrigues, while the other fountain, Fonte da

Rua de São João, dates from the eighteenth century and features a statue of John the Baptist, which the sculptor João Cutileiro added in 2000.

Ponte de Dom Luís I

Largo do Terreiro

MAP p.28, POCKET MAP D8

A short way to the west of the Praça de Ribeira, the attractive square **Largo do Terreiro** leads onto a narrow riverfront path lined with cafés and restaurants with riverfront seating. Most of the houses along this stretch have tunnels (now closed) which once allowed produce to be unloaded straight from the ships.

Ponte de Dom Luís I lower tier

MAP p.28, POCKET MAP F8

Porto's iconic double-decker bridge, **Ponte de Dom Luís I**, was designed by a colleague of Gustav Eiffel (see box, below) and provides one of the city's favourite photo opportunities. You can walk across either level to the port wine lodges, bars and restaurants of Vila Nova de Gaia – traffic runs along the bottom level, while the metro travels across the top level (see p.40). There are steps from the Ribeira up to the lower-level walkway, which lead past a café built on top of the surviving stone piers of an earlier bridge – a great location to stop for a coffee and enjoy an unrivalled view of the bridge and river.

Mind the gap – record-breaking bridges over the Douro

Porto's steep-sided valley has always proved devilishly difficult to traverse. Until 1806, its only crossing was via boats strapped together to form temporary bridges for special occasions. It wasn't until 1843 that the permanent, 170m-span bridge Ponte Pénsil finally crossed the river, and like most of its successors, its span broke world records at the time. In 1877, **Gustave Eiffel** designed the **Ponte Maria Pia** railway bridge, the last major project before he worked on the Eiffel Tower. The Ponte Pénsil was soon replaced by what was then the longest metal arch bridge in the world, the two-tier **Ponte de Dom Luís I**. Designed by Teophile Seyrig, a partner of Eiffel, it opened in 1886 alongside the remaining pillars of the Ponte Pénsil, which you can still see today. There are now six bridges across the Douro in Porto, each a remarkable feat of engineering: in 2003, the **Infante Dom Henrique** bridge at Fontaínhas was opened with the longest concrete arch in the world. The best way to see them all is on one of the many river cruises that depart from either side of the Douro (see box, p.127).

Barredo

Behind the arcades of the Ribeira, the earthy **Barredo** district spreads up the hillside towards the cathedral. The best way to explore this warren of alleys that thumb their noses at the riverside gentrification, is to take the **Ascensor da Ribeira**, a free lift which rises behind the Cais da Ribeira to a rickety platform high above the river. From here, it's an interesting walk back to the riverside: exit the platform at the back (via a few steps) then turn left on the street and you wind down the cobbled lanes. It's about a ten-minute walk back to Ribeira; don't worry if you get lost – that's part of the fun – just keep heading down and you'll hit the riverfront. En route, you'll pass the Torre de Rua de Baixo on the road of the same name, one of the city's oldest surviving tower houses, dating back to the thirteenth century.

Funicular dos Guindais

MAP p.28, POCKET MAP F7
Entrance on Av Gustavo Eifel
ⓦmetrodoporto.pt. Every 10min: April–Oct Mon–Thurs & Sun 8am–10pm, Fri & Sat 8am–midnight; Nov–March Mon–Thurs & Sun 8am–8pm, Fri & Sat 8am–midnight. €2.50 single.

First opened in 1891, and closed two years later following an accident, the **Funicular dos Guindais** is a funicular railway running from the riverfront to Praça da Batalha in just a couple of minutes. The cabins used today date from 2004, when the railway was reopened in time for the Euro 2004 football championships. A trip on the funicular makes for a fun approach to the upper town. The route ascends around 60m, and though it's partly through a tunnel, you can enjoy fine views of the river.

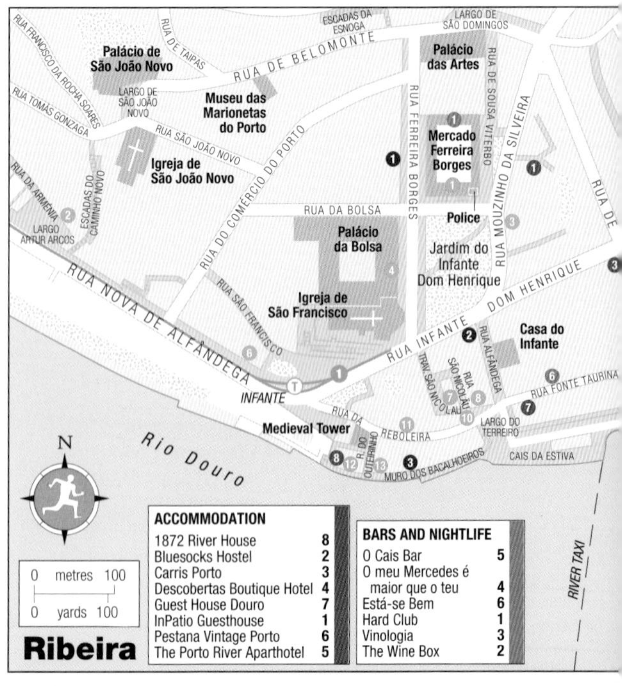

Casa do Infante

MAP p.28, POCKET MAP D7
Rua da Alfândega 10 ⓘ 222 060 435. Tues–Sun 9.30am–1pm & 2–5.30pm, last admission 30min before closing. Museum €2.20; exhibitions often free.

Just back from the central riverside stands the **Casa do Infante**, believed to be the house where Prince Henry the Navigator was born in 1394. Built in 1325 as the Crown's customs house, from 1369 to 1721 it served as part of the Royal Mint. Renovated in the twentieth century, the mansion now serves as a small museum detailing the history of the house, Portugal's maritime discoveries and displaying finds from excavations that revealed the remains of a large Roman palace.

Mercado Ferreira Borges

MAP p.28, POCKET MAP D7
Rua Ferreira Borges ⓘ 220 101 186. Mon–Thurs & Sun 10.30am–midnight, Fri & Sat 10.30am–2am. Free except for special events.

The bright red **Mercado Ferreira Borges** was built in 1885 to replace the old Ribeira market, though the impressive structure didn't function as a market for long and ended up being used as a warehouse. In 2010, the space was given over to the *Hard Club* (see p.35), the *O Mercado* café-restaurant (see p.34) and to operate as a cultural space, but you are free to wander round when events are not being held here. One of the few buildings in Porto built from cast iron, it is considered of extreme architectural importance and faces the attractive Praça do Infante Dom Henrique, a square gathered round a statue of Henry the Navigator, the Portuguese prince who kick-started the country's maritime empire.

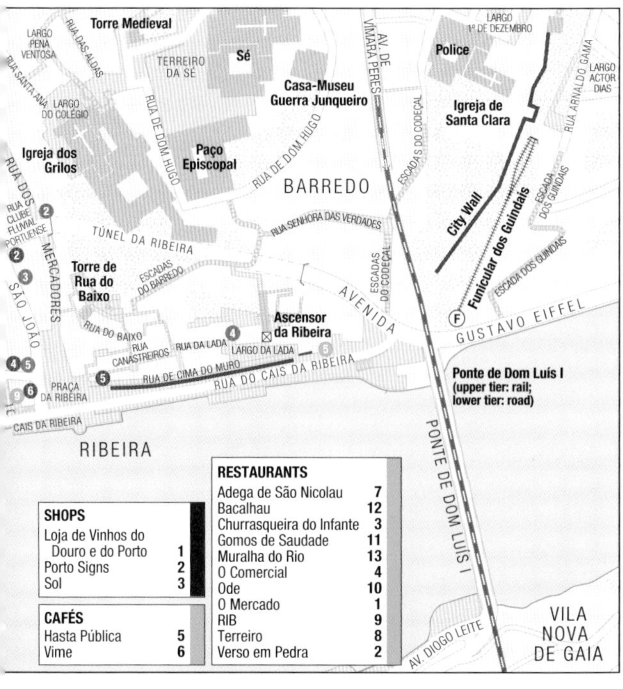

SHOPS	
Loja de Vinhos do Douro e do Porto	1
Porto Signs	2
Sol	3

CAFÉS	
Hasta Pública	5
Vime	6

RESTAURANTS	
Adega de São Nicolau	7
Bacalhau	12
Churrasqueira do Infante	3
Gomos de Saudade	11
Muralha do Rio	13
O Comercial	4
Ode	10
O Mercado	1
RIB	9
Terreiro	8
Verso em Pedra	2

Port

Porto is synonymous with port wine, which you can sample in pretty much every restaurant and bar in the city. It comes in either **ruby** (deep red), **tawny** (made from a blend of differently aged wines) or **white** – the first two are drunk at the end of a meal, the last served chilled as an aperitif. The finest red **vintages** are bottled two to three years after harvest and left to mature. A vintage is only declared in certain years, and the wine is only ready to drink at least ten years after bottling. **Late Bottled Vintage (LBV)** is not of vintage quality, but is still good enough to mature in bottles, to which it's transferred after four to six years in the cask. All other ports are blended and kept in the cask for between two and seven years – then bottled and ready to drink. Of these, a **colheita** ("harvest") is a tawny port aged at least seven years in the cask; other fine wines are **superior tawnies**, between ten and forty years old (the average age of the wines in the blend), while **reserve** ports (both tawny and ruby) are decent blended wines.

Igreja de São Francisco

MAP p.28, POCKET MAP D7
Rua do Infante Dom Henrique ⓣ 222 062 100. Daily: March, April & Oct 9am–7pm; June 9am–7.30pm, July–Sept 9am–8pm; Nov–Feb 9am–6pm. €3.50.

The city's most impressive and only truly **Gothic church**, the fourteenth-century **Igreja de São Francisco** (now deconsecrated), is even more remarkable for what lies within. The interior had a fabulously opulent Rococo makeover in the eighteenth century, with virtually every surface covered in gilded carvings of cherubs, fruit and animals – allegedly 400 kilos of gold were used to decorate it, at a time when Portugal had become rich partly from the gold reserves in its former colony, Brazil. An impressive granite statue of Saint Francis of Assisi is a rare survivor from the original church. Look out for the church's Gothic rose

The catacombs in Igreja de São Francisco

window and for the Tree of Jesse on the north wall, an eighteenth-century sculpture tracing the genealogy of Christ. The other main feature is the **catacombs**, containing thousands of scrubbed human bones. It's an eerie sight for modern sensibilities, but reflects an earlier willingness to confront, and indeed embrace, mortality before the city had public cemeteries.

Palácio da Bolsa

MAP p.28, POCKET MAP D7
Rua Ferreira Borges, at Praça do Infante Dom Henrique ⓣ 223 399 000, ⓦ palaciodabolsa.com. Guided tours (45min) daily: April–Oct 9am–6.30pm; Nov–March 9am–12.30pm & 2–5.30pm. €8.50.

For an indication of the wealth that poured into Porto in the nineteenth century, join a tour of the city's former stock exchange, the **Palácio da Bolsa**, whose interior halls display an almost obscene level of richness. Building started in 1842 in an attempt to encourage traders to invest in the city's commercial enterprises, on the site of the former cloisters of the Igreja de São Francisco, which had burnt down the previous year. Designed by local architect Joaquim da Costa Lima Júnior in the style of a Neoclassical palace, the lavish interior wasn't completed until 1910, and features contributions from various architects and artists. These include the extraordinary **Salão Árabe** – inspired by the Alhambra in Granada – and the **Pátio das Nações**, the original trading floor, which is embellished with the flags of the nations who traded with Portugal at the time. Note, too, the Sala Dourada, which is lined with the portraits of Portugal's presidents and makes for an interesting contrast to the Sala dos Retratos (Picture Hall) with

Palácio da Bolsa

its portraits of the Braganzan kings who ruled before the birth of the republic in 1910. The Bolsa continued to function as a stock exchange until the 1990s, when it merged with the more influential Lisbon stock exchange. You don't need to buy a ticket to see the dramatic iron-, glass-and-tile Pátio das Nações courtyard, a veritable cloister of commerce, whose side rooms contain a craft and jewellery store, wine bar and shop, and the *O Comercial* restaurant (see p.34). But to delve any deeper into the building, you'll have to bear with the rather pricey and fact-heavy guided visits.

Shops

Loja de Vinhos do Douro e do Porto

MAP p.28, POCKET MAP D7
Rua Ferreira Borges 27 ⓣ 222 071 669, ⓦ ivdp.pt. Mon–Fri 11am–7pm.
At the Porto and Douro Wine Institute's central shop and showroom you'll be able to taste a few wines and then buy from the well-stocked shelves. It's also a good place to ask about port wine tours or even to arrange visits to the institute's labs and tasting chambers.

Porto Signs

MAP p.28, POCKET MAP D7
Entrances on Rua Alfandega 17 & Rua Infante Dom Henrique 71 ⓣ 223 745 436, ⓦ portosigns.pt. Daily 10am–8pm.
Good for souvenirs and gifts, this place stocks an interesting array of handicrafts including belts, hats and bags crafted from cork, as well as ceramics, shirts, soaps and toiletries.

Sol

MAP p.28, POCKET MAP D8
Muro dos Bacalhoeiros 125 ⓣ 222 083 956. Daily 10am–6pm.
A fine little cave of a shop that leads back from the riverfront, Sol sells pottery, tiles, mugs, plates and bowls in traditional designs. There's also an original selection of attractive fish-themed wall plaques.

Porto Signs

Cafés

Hasta Pública

MAP p.28, POCKET MAP F7
Cais de Ribeira 20 ⓣ 222 026 001. Mon–Sat 10am–11pm.
A popular café-bar whose tables have terrific views across the bridge and river. It serves a range of inexpensive salads, sandwiches and pizzas (around €8 for a pizza) and also makes a fine stop for a coffee and cake or *pastel de nata*.

Vime

MAP p.28, POCKET MAP C7
Rua Nova de Alfandega 12 ⓣ 222 010 639. Tues–Sun 9am–11pm.
A pleasant, friendly canteen-style café down on the waterfront with great river views through its large windows. The breakfasts are particularly good value – croissant, bread and butter, orange juice and coffee for €4 – and they also serve salads and more hearty dishes, too, such as steak or pork and clams from €9–13. There are a couple of tables outside on the street – but watch out for the trams, which trundle perilously close.

Restaurants

Adega de São Nicolau

MAP p.28, POCKET MAP D8
Rua S. Nicolau 1 ⓣ 222 008 232. Mon–Sat noon–11pm.
Tucked away down an alley just off the Largo do Terreiro, this local place is less touristy than some of its Ribeira neighbours, with a cosy dining room inside plus outdoor tables on a terrace that offers excellent river views. It specializes in good-quality traditional

Portuguese cuisine, with the emphasis on meat and game – try the likes of hare with beans (€15), wild boar (€12.50) or half a roast partridge (€16.50) – though there are also a few fish dishes too. It's small and very popular, so reserve in advance if possible.

Bacalhau

MAP p.28, POCKET MAP D8
Muro dos Bacalheiros 153 ⓣ 222 010 521, ⓦ bacalhauporto.pt. Mon–Thurs & Sun noon–10pm, Fri & Sat noon–11pm.

This classy little restaurant has appealing tables outside on the river wall – they provide blankets in winter – and serves Portuguese cuisine with a contemporary twist. *Bacalhau*, of course, is the main event, in dishes such as rice with cod tongue and chouriço, or turnip greens with *bacalhau* (€14), though there are also meat dishes including ox tongue with peas and potatoes (€13.50).

Churrasqueira do Infante

MAP p.28, POCKET MAP D7
Rua de Mouzinho da Silveira 20 ⓣ 222 000 885. Mon–Sat noon–3.30pm & 6.30–10.30pm.

One of Ribeira's few surviving local restaurants and a good choice if you want a change from the touristy places down on the waterfront. It serves large portions of good-value Portuguese cooking, such as grilled tuna steak (€10), veal escalopes (€7.50) or *arroz de marisco* (€11), all served up without much ceremony.

Gomos de Saudade

MAP p.28, POCKET MAP D8
Rua da Reboleira 36 ⓣ 222 010 404. Mon–Wed & Fri–Sun 10am–midnight.

This titchy backstreet restaurant has spread into a splendidly positioned dining room in the building opposite. The wonderful river views are the draw at what is otherwise a cheap and cheerful place which serves up decent portions of chicken, *pataniscas* (*bacalhau* patties), salmon steaks and fresh fish. The set menu, which includes a soup starter, is good value at around €10.

Muralha do Rio

MAP p.28, POCKET MAP D8
Muro dos Bacalhoeiros 145–146 ⓣ 222 423 264. Daily: May–Sept 11am–10pm; Oct–April 11am–8pm.

A simple restaurant right on the riverfront, with tables outside on the terrace that have fantastic river views. It serves a good-value set lunch menu, that includes soup, a main course such as *bacalhau à bras* (salted cod with potatoes, eggs and olives), a drink and coffee for €12; or go à la carte with dishes such as grilled sea bass for €18. It sometimes puts on fado in the summer too.

A starter for ten euros

At restaurants, don't feel you're being ripped off when you're served an array of starters before you even order your main course, then get a bill for what you've eaten at the end. This is normal practice in Portugal and no waiter will take offence if you politely decline whatever you're offered. Starters can vary from simple bread, butter and olives to prawns, cheeses and cured meats. If you're tempted, it's a good idea to ask the waiter how much each item costs. Check your bill, too, to ensure you've not been charged for anything you declined. Also, watch out for the **portion sizes**. Many restaurants offer dishes in a *meia dose* (half-portion) or a *dose* (portion) – for the vast majority of people a *meia dose* is perfectly adequate and a *dose* is usually enough for two to share.

O Comercial

MAP p.28, POCKET MAP D7
Palácio de Bolsa, Rua Ferreira Borges ☎ 223 322 019. Mon–Fri 12.30–3pm & 7.30–11pm, Sat 7.30–midnight.

Grand arches, towering ceilings and racks of wine set the tone for the restaurant inside the Palácio da Bolsa, the former Porto stock exchange (see p.31). The cuisine offers a modern take on traditional Portuguese dishes, such as octopus with *migas* (a garlicky bread sauce); scallops and prawns with black linguini or steak with foie gras. But despite the quality, you can have this as part of the excellent-value set menu (Mon–Fri only) at just €17 for lunch or €23 for dinner, which includes a starter, main and pudding.

Ode

MAP p.28, POCKET MAP D8
Largo do Terreiro 7 ☎ 913 200 010. Tues–Sun 7–11.30pm.

Part of the slow food movement, *Ode* is small, cosy, stone-clad and exclusive – the sort of place to linger. Mains start from around €22, but the quality is exceptional, featuring the likes of beef in red wine, Alentejan black pork and grilled octopus, all of which can be paired with top Portuguese wines.

O Comercial

O Mercado

MAP p.28, POCKET MAP D7
Mercado Ferreira Borges, Rua Ferreira Borges ☎ 935 274 541. Daily 10.30am–midnight.

On the first floor of the market building (see p.29), this is a wonderful, large and airy space with comfy sofas and big wooden tables (as well as a wood burner in winter). It serves a range of *petiscos*, such as mini kebabs, *francesinhas* and steak sandwiches, as well as tasty wood-fired pizzas, all at €6–10.

RIB

MAP p.28, POCKET MAP E8
Praça da Ribeira 1 ☎ 966 273 822. Daily 12.30–3.30pm & 7.30pm–2am.

A smart riverfront restaurant specializing in meat dishes – if you're not into steak, it's probably not for you (the clue's in the name). While it's not cheap, the food is certainly worth it. Expect to pay up to €40 a person for a three-course meal with wine. Starters include dishes such as egg, truffle and asparagus, and the bar serves excellent cocktails.

Terreiro

MAP p.28, POCKET MAP D8
Largo do Terreiro 11–12 ☎ 222 011 955. Daily noon–11pm.

Highly regarded fish restaurant in a good location with a contemporary interior and tables on the terrace in front that have great views over the river. It specializes in excellent fish and seafood dishes such as clams in onion stew (€14) or hake with cockle rice (€21), plus a variety of simply grilled fresh fish and seafood sold by weight.

Verso em Pedra

MAP p.28, POCKET MAP C7
Rua Armenia 12–16 ☎ 222 058 009. Tues–Sun 11am–2am.

This large, cheap and cheerful café-restaurant serves the usual array of grilled meats, fish and pasta for around €9. However, the main reason to go here is to try its speciality *francesinhas* which come in various types from around €8 – the seafood version with salmon and shrimp (€14) is recommended.

Bars and clubs

O Cais Bar

MAP p.28, POCKET MAP E7
Rua da Fonte Taurina 2 ⓣ 918 397 217. Daily 2pm–1am.

Steps lead down to this relaxed bar with a clientele as varied as the soundtrack. Serves *petiscos*, foreign beers and mojitos, with frequent football on the TVs inside. There are also a few outside tables for when it gets hot.

O meu Mercedes é maior que o teu

MAP p.28, POCKET MAP E7
Rua da Lada 30 ⓣ 222 082 151. Mon–Thurs 8pm–1am, Fri & Sat 8pm–4am.

The stalwart of the Ribeira scene not only wins the Porto bar best name prize ("My Mercedes is bigger than yours") but it's also an atmospheric joint to boot, a bit like an old stone-walled wine cellar. It's a great place for a drink, and also lays on regular rock gigs.

Está-se Bem

MAP p.28, POCKET MAP D8
Rua da Fonte Taurina 70–72 ⓣ 222 900 900. Tues–Sun noon–midnight.

A cute little backstreet tapas bar serving a range of cocktails and snacks such as octopus with red peppers, tripe and *pregos* (€1–6).

Hard Club

MAP p.28, POCKET MAP D7
Mercado Ferreira Borges, Praça do Infante Dom Henrique ⓣ 220 101 186, ⓦ facebook .com/HardClubPorto. Mon–Thurs & Sun 10.30am–midnight, Fri & Sat 10.30am–2am.

In the main hall of the Mercado Ferreira Borges (see p.29), this

The Wine Box

is a huge space that can hold up to a thousand people. It's a great venue for regular events, exhibitions, club nights and concerts: check the website for what's on.

Vinologia

MAP p.28, POCKET MAP E7
Rua de São João 46 ⓣ 912 538 219. Daily 11am–midnight.

This is an alluring bar with big wooden tables where you can sample a range of ports from some of the lesser-known producers. Start with a basic port at around €4 a glass, or push the boat out with a €65 glass of Tawny Calheita dating back to the 1960s. The staff are friendly and knowledgeable.

The Wine Box

MAP p.28, POCKET MAP E7
Rua dos Mercadores 72 ⓣ 222 034 100. Mon & Thurs–Sun 10am–midnight, Tues–Wed 3pm–midnight.

Despite its position right next to the entrance of a road tunnel, this is a fashionable, modern space which does a fine range of wines and tapas, such as tuna with pepper, bacon and pineapple and *pica pau* (spicy sausage with a cheesy sauce), all around €4–7.

The Sé, Aliados and northern Porto

Some of Porto's oldest and most atmospheric streets are tightly knitted into the steep slopes below the Sé, Porto's ancient cathedral which looms high above the Douro. Here you'll find the Paço Episcopal, the ornate palace of the bishops of Porto, and nearby, some of Porto's most impressive churches: Igreja de Santa Clara and Igreja de Santo Ildefonso. From below the old city walls the top tier of the Ponte de Dom Luís I offers a dramatic approach to the river's south side, while north of the Sé lie the fabulously tiled São Bento train station, the grand town hall at the top of the main square, Aliados, and the vibrant Bolhão market. North of here, the Estádio do Dragão, the famed home of FC Porto, is the main point of interest.

Sé

MAP p.38, POCKET MAP E6–E7
Terreiro da Sé ⓣ 222 059 028. Cathedral daily: April–Oct 9am–12.30pm & 2.30–7pm; Nov–March 9am–12.30pm & 2.30–6pm. Free. Cloisters daily: April–Oct 9am–12.15pm & 2.30–6.30pm; Nov–March Mon–Sat 9am–12.15pm & 2.30–5.30pm. Cloisters, Sala Capitular and Tesouro €3.

Porto's impressive hulk of a cathedral, the **Sé**, commands the eastern heights above the river. Construction started in the twelfth century and its austere exterior is a reminder that at the time, it was a defiant and resilient structure built not long after the Moorish occupation of the area and just a few years after Portugal had become an independent country. The building has been greatly enlarged and developed since the original Gothic structure. On the north tower (the one with the bell), look for the very worn bas-relief depicting a fourteenth-century ship – a reminder of Portugal's (and Porto's) maritime past. Despite its great age, there's no real sense of majesty inside the cathedral, with the altar and chapels making little impact in the darkness. The **cloisters**, however, are a different matter, their arched walls filled with magnificent Baroque *azulejos* designed by Valentim de Almeida in around 1730. Italian architect Nicolau Nasoni, the designer of many of Porto's grand eighteenth-century buildings (see box, p.51), added an impressive, granite staircase, which climbs from the cloisters to the restored **Sala Capitular** (Chapter Room), with more *azulejos*, painted ceiling panels and views from the shuttered windows. In the **Tesouro** (Treasury), meanwhile, is the usual boggling array of silver and gold – beautifully lit for once.

Paço Episcopal

MAP p.38, POCKET MAP E7
Terreiro da Sé ⓣ 223 392 330. Mon, Tues & Thurs–Sat 9am–1pm & 2–6pm. 30min tours every 30min. €5.

To the south side of the Sé stretches the grandiose frontage of the **Paço Episcopal**, the archbishop's palace. The bishops of Porto first took up residence here in the thirteenth

Sé

century, and it was here that the first king of Portugal was crowned (and spent his wedding night) – only a small window by the main entrance survives from this time. Most of today's structure dates to the eighteenth century when it was largely rebuilt by Nicolau Nasoni (see box, p.51), and gives an idea of the bishops' luxurious lifestyle. Construction started in 1772, but took nearly 100 years. Initially the bishop didn't approve of Nasoni's design; later, in the 1830s, the palace was badly damaged during the Portuguese civil war and it wasn't until 1871 that it was finally completed. The result is a mish-mash of architectural elements: a Rococo stairway lined with carved granite flowers, Neoclassical doorways and Baroque decorations. The tour takes you around all but the bishop's private quarters, the rooms filled with priceless furniture (such as seventeenth-century Indo-Portuguese cabinets) and works of art, including portraits of all the Bishops of Portugal. The palace served as Porto's town hall from the birth of the republic in 1911 to 1956, when the archbishop moved back in – ironically, most of the religious paintings here date from this era. There are great views from the front balconies.

Casa-Museu Guerra Junqueiro

MAP p.38, POCKET MAP E6–F7
Rua de Dom Hugo 32 ⓣ 222 003 689. Mon–Sat 10am–5.30pm, Sun 10am–12.30pm & 2–5.30pm (last entry 30mins before closing). €3.

With its entrance behind Porto's cathedral, the **Casa-Museu Guerra Junqueiro** is the Baroque eighteenth-century mansion where the poet, writer and politician Abílio Manuel Guerra Junqueiro (1850–1923) used to live and write his famous works, which reflected the revolutionary turmoil of the Republican era. He spent his lifetime collecting Iberian and Islamic art, and the rooms here recapture the atmosphere of the era with displays of ceramics, glassware, glazed earthenware, jewellery and textiles. The mansion, which was built to a design attributed to Nasoni (see box, p.51) also hosts an active calendar of events, including fado performances and poetry readings.

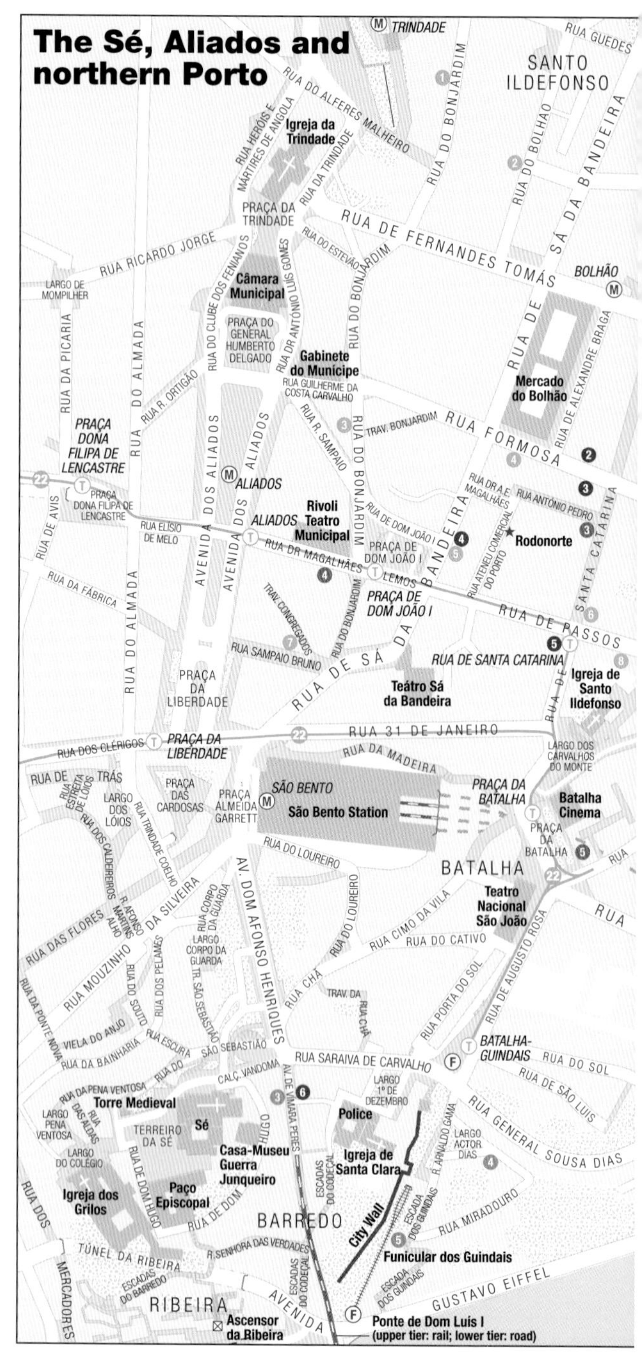
The Sé, Aliados and northern Porto
TRINDADE
SANTO ILDEFONSO
BOLHÃO
ALIADOS
SÃO BENTO
BATALHA
BATALHA-GUINDAIS
BARREDO
RIBEIRA
Igreja da Trindade
Câmara Municipal
Gabinete do Munícipe
Mercado do Bolhão
Rivoli Teatro Municipal
Rodonorte
Teátro Sá da Bandeira
Igreja de Santo Ildefonso
São Bento Station
Batalha Cinema
Teatro Nacional São João
Torre Medieval
Sé
Casa-Museu Guerra Junqueiro
Paço Episcopal
Igreja dos Grilos
Police
Igreja de Santa Clara
City Wall
Funicular dos Guindais
Ascensor da Ribeira
Ponte de Dom Luís I (upper tier: rail; lower tier: road)
PRAÇA DONA FILIPA DE LENCASTRE
PRAÇA DE DOM JOÃO I
PRAÇA DA LIBERDADE
PRAÇA DA BATALHA
RUA DE FERNANDES TOMÁS
RUA FORMOSA
RUA DE PASSOS MANUEL
RUA DE SANTA CATARINA
RUA 31 DE JANEIRO
RUA DOS CLÉRIGOS
AVENIDA DOS ALIADOS
RUA DE SÁ DA BANDEIRA
AV. DOM AFONSO HENRIQUES
RUA DAS FLORES
RUA MOUZINHO DA SILVEIRA
GUSTAVO EIFFEL

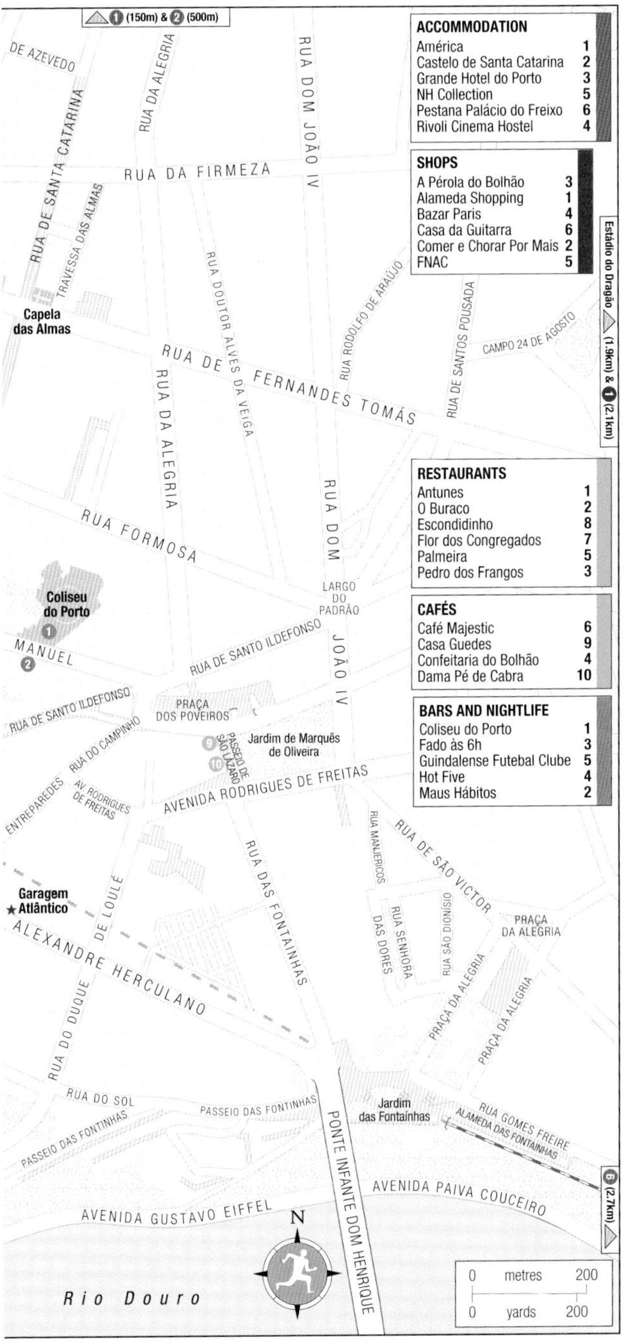

(150m) & (500m)
ACCOMMODATION
América 1
Castelo de Santa Catarina 2
Grande Hotel do Porto 3
NH Collection 5
Pestana Palácio do Freixo 6
Rivoli Cinema Hostel 4
SHOPS
A Pérola do Bolhão 3
Alameda Shopping 1
Bazar Paris 4
Casa da Guitarra 6
Comer e Chorar Por Mais 2
FNAC 5
Estádio do Dragão (1.9km) & (2.1km)
RESTAURANTS
Antunes 1
O Buraco 2
Escondidinho 8
Flor dos Congregados 7
Palmeira 5
Pedro dos Frangos 3
CAFÉS
Café Majestic 6
Casa Guedes 9
Confeitaria do Bolhão 4
Dama Pé de Cabra 10
BARS AND NIGHTLIFE
Coliseu do Porto 1
Fado às 6h 3
Guindalense Futebal Clube 5
Hot Five 4
Maus Hábitos 2
DE AZEVEDO
RUA DA ALEGRIA
RUA DOM JOÃO IV
RUA DE SANTA CATARINA
RUA DA FIRMEZA
TRAVESSA DAS ALMAS
RUA DOUTOR ALVES DA VEIGA
RUA RODOLFO DE ARAÚJO
RUA DE SANTOS POUSADA
CAMPO 24 DE AGOSTO
Capela das Almas
RUA DE FERNANDES TOMÁS
RUA DA ALEGRIA
RUA FORMOSA
RUA DOM JOÃO IV
LARGO DO PADRÃO
Coliseu do Porto
MANUEL
RUA DE SANTO ILDEFONSO
RUA DE SANTO ILDEFONSO
PRAÇA DOS POVEIROS
RUA DO CAMPINHO
PASSEIO DE SÃO LÁZARO
Jardim de Marquês de Oliveira
ENTREPAREDES
AV. RODRIGUES DE FREITAS
AVENIDA RODRIGUES DE FREITAS
RUA MANJERICOS
RUA DE SÃO VICTOR
RUA DAS FONTAINHAS
Garagem Atlântico
DE LOULÉ
ALEXANDRE HERCULANO
RUA SENHORA DAS DORES
RUA SÃO DIONÍSIO
PRAÇA DA ALEGRIA
PRAÇA DA ALEGRIA
PRAÇA DA ALEGRIA
RUA DO DUQUE
RUA DO SOL
PASSEIO DAS FONTINHAS
PASSEIO DAS FONTINHAS
Jardim das Fontaínhas
RUA GOMES FREIRE
ALAMEDA DAS FONTAINHAS
PONTE INFANTE DOM HENRIQUE
(2.7km)
AVENIDA PAIVA COUCEIRO
AVENIDA GUSTAVO EIFFEL
N
Rio Douro
0 metres 200
0 yards 200

Terreiro da Sé

MAP p.38, POCKET MAP E7

The broad **Terreiro da Sé** is one of Porto's largest squares and the view from the terrace is superb, looking down over old-town streets tumbling down towards the Douro. Although it's surrounded by ancient buildings, the square was actually laid out in the 1940s when the Estado Novo (the regime under the dictator Salazar) decided to clear away some of the medieval buildings to create a public space. In the square there's the distinctive Pelourinho da Sé, an ornately twisted column which was also placed here in the 1940s, though based on a design dating back to 1797. Just below the square you'll see a medieval tower house, now home to a small tourist office (see p.126). The tower was actually reconstructed in the 1940s and features a Gothic balcony. Continue downhill from here and you'll pass through the warren of streets, steps and alleys that make up the Barredo district (see p.28), where locals live cheek-by-jowl as they have done for centuries.

Ponte de Dom Luís I top tier

Ponte de Dom Luís I top tier

MAP p.38, POCKET MAP F8

To the east of the Sé, Avenida de Vimara Peres leads down to the top tier of the spectactular **Ponte de Dom Luís I** (see p.27 for the bottom tier). Originally built for cars and buses, the top tier is now used by the Porto metro (take the Santo Ovídio line and this section is between the stops of São Bento and Jardim do Morro), and you can also walk across it for stunning views over the town and the Douro. Continue over the bridge for easy access to the monastery of Serra do Pilar in Vila Nova da Gaia (see p.61), or the port wine lodges via the cable car (see p.64).

Igreja de Santa Clara

MAP p.38, POCKET MAP F7

Largo Primeiro Dezembro ⓣ 223 392 330. Mon–Fri 10am–12.30pm & 2.30–5pm, Sat 10am–12.30pm. Free.

Dating back to the fifteenth century and with a distinctive Renaissance portal, the **Igreja de Santa Clara** was rebuilt in the eighteenth century and, at the time of writing, was undergoing renovation (and might be closed periodically as a result). Entered through a courtyard, the interior is a dazzling ensemble of ornate gilded wood. The restoration project is one of the most important being undertaken by the Porto School of Wood Carvers, who are gradually cleaning up the somewhat faded but still exuberant gold leaf that covers almost every surface of the walls and ceiling. A grill separates the church from an adjacent convent, which is now used by the police.

Igreja de Santo Ildefonso

MAP p.38, POCKET MAP G5

Praça da Batalha ⓣ 222 004 366. Mon–Sat 8.30am–6.30pm, Sun 9am–7. Free.

Another impressive church is the

Igreja de Santo Ildefonso, which rises above the Praça da Batalha. The beautiful *azulejos* that adorn the facade were designed in the 1930s by Jorge Calaço – who was responsible for the São Bento station's tiles (see p.42) – though the church, with two distinct bell towers, dates back to the eighteenth century. It was from here that the attempted revolution in 1891 was seen off by municipal guards, who forced the attacking republicans to retreat and eventually surrender from their position at the top of the church steps.

Teatro Nacional São João

MAP p.38, POCKET MAP G6
Praça da Batalha Ⓣ 223 401 900, Ⓦ www.tnsj.pt. Ticket office open Tues–Sat 2–7pm, Sun 2–5pm.

Inspired by Charles Garnier's Opera house in Paris, the **Teatro Nacional São João** is a gorgeously over-the-top building, built in 1911 to replace an earlier theatre which was destroyed in a fire. Today the city's major theatre and opera venue for Portuguese and international productions, it was renovated in the 1990s after having served as a cinema since the 1930s. The programme is pretty varied and you can see a show for as little as €7.50.

Jardim de Marquês de Oliveira

MAP p.38, POCKET MAP H5
Entrance on Passeio de São Lázaro. Daily: April–Sept 9am–8pm, Oct–March 9am–7pm. Free.

Tucked away off the tourist route, the attractive **Jardim de Marquês de Oliveira** is a lovely space where elderly men gather to play cards under the shade of beautiful magnolia, linden and cedar trees. The gardens were laid out in 1833 on the site of a former leper colony and formed the city's first-ever public gardens, dotted with fountains and statues, centred around a little lake. Unusually for Portugal, the gardens are railed off and closed at night.

The Linha do Douro

Trains depart daily from São Bento station (full timetable on Ⓦ cp.pt) along the **Linha do Douro**. One of the most beautiful rail routes in Europe, the Linha do Douro follows the banks of the Douro river valley right into the heart of the dramatic terraces of the port wine-growing estates. A true engineering marvel when it opened in 1887, the Linha do Douro still thrills passengers today. In its heyday it crossed the border to Spain (for a through service to Salamanca and Madrid) and sprouted some stunning valley branch lines, but even though these branches are no more, it's a fantastic ride – 160km of river-hugging track from Porto to Pocinho, via more than 20 tunnels, 30 bridges and 34 stations. You change onto the smaller Douro Line trains at Peso da Régua (just "Régua" on timetables), which at around two hours from Porto, is a manageable day-trip. However, **Régua** also marks the point at which the Douro Line turns from a good route into a great one, sticking closely to the river from then on, clinging to the precipitous rocks as the river – and track – passes through the Douro gorge. Some of the stations are no more than a shelter on a platform, used by the local wine *quintas*, though there are useful stops at **Pinhão** (a pretty port-producing town), **Tua** (a cruise halt with a good restaurant) and finally the relatively titchy and nondescript **Pocinho** (around three and half hours' journey time, making a long day-trip just about feasible).

São Bento Station

MAP p.38, POCKET MAP F5
Praça Almeida Garrett.

It is not often that a train station concourse is a sight in its own right, but the one at **São Bento** is one of the most beautiful in the world. Built on the site of a former convent in 1900, it is decorated with around 20,000 sumptuous *azulejos* by painter Jorge Colaço. These show various scenes from Portuguese history, including the visit of Dom João I to Porto in 1387, with his wife Philippa of Lancaster. The towering, ornate ceilings, arched windows and impressive clock all give the appearance of a palace ballroom rather than a ticket hall. In 2016, Time Out applied to use the space to house a Porto version of their successful Lisbon market, but the mayor turned down the request as unsuitable for such a historic space. The station is the starting point for the fantastic Linha do Douro (see box, p.41).

Avenida dos Aliados

MAP p.38, POCKET MAP E4–F4

Not quite all roads lead to the **Avenida dos Aliados** (just "Aliados" to locals), but most do. At the foot of the broad avenue – in the area known as Praça da Liberdade – are a couple of pavement cafés and an equestrian statue of Dom Pedro IV; at the head stands the statue of celebrated local boy Almeida Garrett (1799–1854), poet, novelist, dramatist and Liberal politician. Behind the statue at the top of the avenue is Porto's city hall, the **Câmara Municipal**, whose 70m-high clock tower sits at the top of the square. The town hall was designed in 1914 but didn't open until the 1950s. To the left of the town hall as you face it is the city's main tourist office (see p.126).

Capela das Almas

Mercado do Bolhão

MAP p.38, POCKET MAP G3–G4
Rua Formosa. Mon–Fri 7am–5pm, Sat 7am–1pm.

The heartbeat of the busy commercial area around Rua Formosa is the wrought-iron **Mercado do Bolhão**. Built in 1914 and set on two levels, the market has a balcony running round the top that gives it a theatrical air as you peer down over the bustle of stalls. There's been a market on this spot since 1839 and, it feels little changed since then, with stalls selling beans by weight, fishmongers gutting their fish in front of you and cages of live chickens, rabbits and pigeons. The market building itself has been neglected for years and is very run-down – as a result, substantial renovation is planned, with the upper storey becoming a space for shops, restaurants and events, and the ground floor housing traditional stalls. Work has begun and is due to be completed in 2019.

Capela das Almas

MAP p.38, POCKET MAP G3
Rua de Santa Catarina 428 ⓣ 222 005 765. Daily 8am–6.30pm. Free.

Also known as the chapel of Santa Catarina, the most striking aspect of the early eighteenth-century **Capela das Almas** is its exterior,

Porto's azulejos

Porto has some of Portugal's best **azulejos** – decorative ceramic tiles – and you can see a variety of styles decorating houses, shops, monuments and churches all over the city. The craft was brought over by the Moors in the eighth century. Portuguese *azulejos* developed their own style around the mid-sixteenth century when a new Italian technique enabled images to be painted directly onto the clay, thanks to a tin oxide coating which prevented running.

Wealthy Portuguese began to commission large *azulejo* panels displaying battles and fantastic images influenced by Vasco da Gama's voyages to the East. The early eighteenth century saw highly trained artists producing elaborate multicoloured **ceramic mosaics**, often with Rococo or Baroque themes as in the interior of the Sé (see p.36). After the Great Earthquake, more prosaic tiled facades, often with **Neoclassical designs**, were considered good insulation devices, as well as protecting buildings from rain and fire. After the mid-nineteenth century, *azulejos* were being mass-produced to decorate shops and religious buildings, such as the fantastic exterior of the Igreja do Carmo (see p.52). By the 1900s, Portugal had become the world's leading producer of *azulejos*, with Art Deco designs taking hold in the 1920s – witness the facade of the Pérola do Bolhão shop (see p.44). São Bento station's entrance hall (see opposite) represents a coming together of all the best that *azulejos* have to offer, a panoply of panels designed in the 1930s by Jorge Calaço representing key scenes in the country's development. Also worth seeking out is the Capela das Almas (see opposite), whose images depicting the lives of the saints are an early twentieth-century recreation of eighteenth-century designs.

which is lined with *azulejos* showing scenes from the death of St Francis of Assissi and the Martyrdom of St Catherine. The tiles were designed in 1929 by artist and ceramicist Eduardo Leite, but mimic the style of *azulejos* that were popular in the eighteenth century. There are also stained-glass windows, nineteenth-century embellishments by Amandio Silva.

Estádio do Dragão

MAP p.38

Via Futebal Clube do Porto, Antas, off Av Fernão Magalhães Ⓜ Estádio do Dragão Ⓣ 707 281 893, Ⓦ fcporto.pt. Tours (45min): Mon at 3pm, 4pm & 5pm; Tues–Sun 11am, noon, 1pm, 2pm, 3pm, 4pm & 5pm. €15 including museum; €12 on match days when the tour doesn't include the stadium. Shop: daily 10am–7pm.

The impressive 50,400-capacity **Estádio do Dragão**, 4km northeast of the centre, is home to FC Porto, European champions in 2004 and winners of the Europa League in 2011 (see p.126). Built for the 2004 European Championships, it's a great match venue and rarely sells out. Tickets cost €15–60, and are available from the club website, the East Stand ticket office or from various shops in town; see website for details. The stadium also hosts major gigs, with Coldplay and the Rolling Stones having played here. You can visit the ground on tours, which leave from outside the club museum. The museum is fascinating if you have an interest in the club's history. You can see FC Porto's array of trophies and watch recordings of past glories, and learn about the club's formation in 1893 by a local wine trader.

A Pérola do Bolhão

Shops

A Pérola do Bolhão

MAP p.38, POCKET MAP G4
Rua Formosa 279 ⓣ 222 004 009. Mon–Sat 7am–8pm.

This great little grocery-cum-café was founded in 1917 and is loved as much for its Art Nouveau facade and its colourful *azulejos* as it is for its rather cluttered stock of goods ranging from *bacalhau* and port wine to mountain cheeses, cured sausages and smoked hams.

Alameda Shopping

MAP p.38
Rua dos Campeões Europeus 28–198 Ⓜ Estádio do Dragão ⓣ 225 076 280, ⓦ alamedashopping.pt. Mon–Thurs & Sun 10am–11pm, Fri–Sat 10am–midnight.

Located close to FC Porto's stadium, this giant modern shopping centre is set over five floors with more than 120 shops, including a Continente hypermarket, a seven-screen cinema, a free car park and various restaurants. There are local and international shops including Bertrand bookshop, Imaginarium toys, Lacoste, Levi and Mango, Benetton, Zara and Sport Zone.

Bazar de Paris

MAP p.38, POCKET MAP F4
Rua Sá da Bandeira 190 ⓣ 222 004 048. Mon–Sat 10am–7pm.

This small and rather unassuming place is the oldest toy shop in the city, and is a good place to find a combination of the usual range of kids' toys and games along with some lovely vintage retro toys including dolls, cars and train sets.

Casa da Guitarra

MAP p.38, POCKET MAP F6
Av Vímara Peres 72 ⓣ 222 010 033, ⓦ casadaguitarra.pt. Mon–Sat 10am–1pm & 2.30–7pm.

Situated on the road leading to the top tier of Ponte de Dom Luís I, this space sells and produces an array of beautiful Portuguese guitars, and by doing so is working to maintain an ancient craft. The shop also promotes music lessons, exhibitions as well as the *Fado às 6h* concerts (see p.47).

Comer e Chorar Por Mais

MAP p.38, POCKET MAP G4
Rua Formosa 300 ⓣ 222 004 407. Mon–Fri 9am–7.30pm, Sat 9am–7pm.

This shop's name translates as "Eat and cry for Mum" and you will be more than tempted to do the former here: this is a treasure trove of tasty things to eat, from their selection of ripe cheeses and smoked and cured sausages, to delicious ports, wines and preserves.

FNAC

MAP p.38, POCKET MAP G5
Rua de Santa Catarina 73 ⓦ fnac.pt. Mon–Sat 10am–8pm, Sun noon–8pm.

This is the most central branch of this large department store chain. and is the one to head to for the city's biggest selection of CDs, DVDs, books, games and other gizmos.

Cafés

Café Majestic

MAP p.38, POCKET MAP G4
Rua de Santa Catarina 112 ⓣ 222 003 887, ⓦ cafemajestic.com. Mon–Sat 9.30am–midnight.

The best-known of the city's *belle époque* cafés, with perfectly preserved decor (celestial cherubs, bevelled mirrors, carved chairs and wood panelling) and waiters with braided hair flitting about to the strains of *The Blue Danube*. Come for coffee or afternoon tea – or maybe have a Caesar salad, club sandwich or *francesinha* for lunch (snacks from €6, mains €13–20), though you may have to wait for a table at busy times.

Casa Guedes

MAP p.38, POCKET MAP H5
Praça dos Poveiros 130 ⓣ 222 002 874. Mon–Sat 8am–midnight.

This tiny, atmospheric, no-frills, tiled café serves some of Porto's tastiest roast pork sandwiches. Queue up at the counter to pre-pay, then watch as slabs of juicy pork are piled onto a bread roll – and topped with melted cheese, too, if you want – then head outside to sit at one of the tables looking onto the square. A sandwich and drink for two costs under €10, or opt for the good-value dish-of-the-day, such as roast veal for €6.

Confeitaria do Bolhão

MAP p.38, POCKET MAP G4
Rua Formosa 339 ⓣ 223 395 220. Daily 6am–8pm.

Opposite Bolhão market, this wonderful, bustling café, deli and shop dates back to 1896. The counter is laden with cakes and pasties, such as *pão de deu* (a sweet bread), onion cake and giant *pastel de nata*. It also serves good-value daily set lunches from around €7.50.

Dama Pé de Cabra

MAP p.38, POCKET MAP H5
Passeio de Sao Lazaro 5 ⓣ 22 3 196 776. Tues–Thurs 9.30am–3.30pm, Fri & Sat 9.30am–3.30pm & 7–11pm.

Looking onto the pretty Jardim de Marques de Oliveira, the oddly named "Woman with a goat's foot" is a great spot for breakfast, lunch or brunch. They make their own breads, featuring ingredients such as chestnut, pumpkin and carrot, which you can enjoy at breakfast toasted with eggs or homemade jam, or served in a variety of sandwiches (from €3) for lunch.

Restaurants

Antunes

MAP p.38, POCKET MAP F2
Rua do Bonjardim 525–529 ⓣ 222 052 406. Mon–Sat noon–3pm & 7–10pm; closed four weeks in Aug/Sept.

This small local restaurant serves traditional dishes, such as fantastic meat stews, roast pork, hake with rice and decent steaks (mains around €9). If you add a dessert and a carafe of house *rosado*, you'll eat well for around €15.

Café Majestic

O Buraco

MAP p.38, POCKET MAP G3
Rua do Bolhão 95 ⓣ 222 006 717. Mon–Fri noon–3.30pm & 4–11pm, Sat noon–6pm.

This is a good-value, no-nonsense local where you can enjoy solid portions of veal, pork, *alheira* and other meaty treats, as well as fresh fish and a fine *arroz de pato* (duck rice), all from around €6–8.

Escondidinho

MAP p.38, POCKET MAP G5
Rua Passos Manuel 142 ⓣ 222 001 079. Daily noon–3pm & 7–11pm.

Its name means "little hidden one", but with its ornate tiled entrance hall it's hardly inconspicuous. This upmarket restaurant is little changed from when it opened in the 1930s, full of wood beams and ceramics. The speciality here is *cataplana*: choose from meat, fish, seafood or a mix (€30 for two). There's also grilled fish and meats, plus some veggie dishes. Prices start at €15, which is good value since past guests have included Spanish and Italian royalty, plus famous Portuguese prime ministers Mario Soares and Sá Carneiro.

Flor dos Congregados

MAP p.38, POCKET MAP F5
Trav dos Congredados 11 ⓣ 222 002 822. Mon–Wed 7–11pm, Thurs–Sat noon–3pm & 7–11pm.

Located down a small back alley, this restaurant dates back to 1852 and claims to have used 1001 traditional recipes. Inside, its stone walls and cosy ambience are as appealing as the menu, chalked up on boards and featuring the likes of tripe, game sausage, tuna steaks and sea bass, from €10–15.

Palmeira

MAP p.38, POCKET MAP F4
Rua Ateneu Comercial do Porto 36 ⓣ 220 055 601. Daily noon–10pm.

Handy if you're catching a bus from the Rodonorte bus station opposite, this bustling local has a long menu of good-value fish and meat (*bacalhau*, *pescada*, roast lamb, *alheira* sausage etc.) from around €8. Join the locals on stools at the bar or take a seat in the larger dining room downstairs.

Pedro dos Frangos

MAP p.38, POCKET MAP F4
Rua do Bonjardim 223 & 312 ⓣ 222 004 882. Daily noon–11pm.

Places specializing in chargrilled chicken are scarce in central Porto, but this place has been serving bargain *frango na brasa* since the 1950s, served with a generous helping of chips and salad. Half a chicken is around €6, and you can also order octopus, steaks and other grills for under €10. The restaurant spreads to both sides of the road: both parts have an upstairs dining

Porto's specialities

Porto's menus go big on grilled fish, seafood and *bacalhau*, but the most authentic local speciality is *tripas* (tripe) – the story goes that the inhabitants selflessly gave away all their meat for Infante Dom Henrique's expeditions to North Africa, leaving themselves only the tripe, and it's been on the menu ever since, cooked *à moda do Porto* (stewed with chouriço and white beans). The other speciality is the **francesinha** ("little French thing") – a mighty chunk of steak, sausage and ham between toasted bread, covered with melted cheese and a peppery tomato-and-beer sauce. It was invented by a café worker called Daniel Silva, who had lived in France and decided to do his own version of their croque monsieur. Don't plan on doing anything much after chowing down on either of these Porto belt-tighteners.

room and a downstairs bar area. The original branch is at no.223.

Bars and live music venues

Coliseu do Porto

MAP p.38, POCKET MAP G5
Rua de Passos Manuel 137 ⓣ 223 394 940, ⓦ coliseudoporto.pt. Ticket office open Aug Mon–Fri 3–7pm, Sept–July Mon–Sat 1–8.30pm.

The main city-centre venue for international acts, with shows ranging from rock, indie and pop to ballet, classical and musicals.

Fado às 6h

MAP p.38, POCKET MAP F6
Av Vímara Peres 49 ⓣ 222 010 033, ⓦ casadaguitarra.pt. Thurs–Sat at 6pm, €10.

Organized by the Casa da Guitarra (see p.44), these live "fado at 6" performances are a good introduction to this distinctive Portuguese music. The concerts are just over an hour, in a small, intimate venue, and include a glass of port in the interval. They often feature performances and workshops by top fado guitarists such as Cústodio Castelo.

Guindalense Futebal Clube

MAP p.38, POCKET MAP F7
Escadas dos Guindais 43 ⓣ 222 034 246. Daily 2pm–midnight.

Begun in 1976 by a group of boys who liked playing football (and are still active in promoting sport amongst young people), the community-run *Guindalense FC* has a lively cafe-bar, with a series of terraces and fantastic views over the river and Ponte de Dom Luís I. Head inside for a game of pool, or outside on the terraces where you can play babyfoot or just sit watching the metro trundling across the bridge. It's always busy

Guindalense Futebal Clube

with students and young people who come for the convivial atmosphere, great views and cheap food and beer (a *tosta* and beer costs €3), and has occasional evening dance nights.

Hot Five

MAP p.38, POCKET MAP G7
Largo do Actor Dias 51 ⓣ 934 328 583, ⓦ hotfive.pt. Wed–Sat 10pm–3am.

Long-established and charismatic jazz club close to the top of the Elevador de Guindais. There are live acts most nights, and though jazz and blues are the staples, they also showcase local talent in different genres. There are two bar areas decorated with black and white photos of jazz legends.

Maus Hábitos

MAP p.38, POCKET MAP G5
Rua Passos Manuel 178–4° ⓣ 222 087 268, ⓦ maushabitos.com. Restaurant Mon–Fri 12.30–3pm; gallery Wed–Sun 10pm–2am; bar Wed, Thurs & Sun 10pm–2am, Fri & Sat 10pm–4am.

At the top of an Art Deco car park is "Bad Habits", a late-night, in-crowd venue for alternative music (jazz, funk, indie and world) and contemporary arts. It's not as exclusively hip as you might expect, and out-of-towners are more than welcome – coming for the daily veggie lunch is a good way for a first look around, and then you can check out what's coming up and what's on in the gallery.

The Baixa

Although Baixa means "lower town", Porto's commercial heart lies well above the riverfront. Its main sights are the ornate Igreja do Carmo church, famed for its dazzling azulejos tiles; the city's best vantage point in the form of the towering Torre dos Clérigos; and the Centro Português de Fotografia, whose location in a former prison is every bit as fascinating as its exhibits. A lively, bustling district that is fun simply to wander around, the Baixa is home to the city's university and has its fair share of cafés, bars, clubs and shops, including one of Europe's most visited bookshops, the over-the-top Livraria Lello, put firmly on the tourist map by former customer, J K Rowling.

Museu da Misericórdia do Porto

MAP p.49, POCKET MAP D6
Rua das Flores 15 ⓣ 220 906 960, ⓦ mmipo.pt. Daily: April–Sept 10am–6.30pm; Oct–March 10am–5.30pm. €5; guided tours €1 extra.

Adjoining the stunning sixteenth-century Igreja da Misericórdia church, this surprisingly interesting **museum**, spread over four floors, was completely remodelled in 2015 and won the award for the Portuguese museum of the year in 2016. Until 2013, the building was home to the Santa Casa da Misericórdia, one of the country's oldest and largest charitable organizations, which was founded over five hundred years ago for philanthropic purposes. The museum's top floor traces the history of the organization, which funded and ran hospitals for the poor, paid for surgeons and lawyers for prisoners, and also built the first orphanage, installed a Braille press for the blind and built a medical school in Porto: look out for the display cabinets housing some of the medical school's original surgical instruments, such as a primitive brain-surgery kit and horrific-looking electric shock therapy equipment. There's also an impressive Gallery of Benefactors, containing paintings of those who provided funds for the charity – the size of each painting corresponds to how much the subject in it donated. The second floor displays the organization's rich collection of religious art, including paintings, sculptures, ornate gold and silver reliquaries, jewellery and vestments embroidered with gold thread – the scale of the treasures gives some idea of the Misericórdia's wealth at its prime. The highlight of the first floor is the *Fons Vitae*, a huge painting by an unknown artist of the Flemish School (around 1520) showing Dom Manuel I with his family kneeling before Christ on the cross. A beautiful iron and glass gallery with a tiled floor leads into the choir of the impressive Baroque Igreja da Misericórdia, which was largely rebuilt in the eighteenth century by Nicolau Nasoni (see box, p.51). Access to the main chapel, with its stunning tiled nave and beautiful sacristry, is on the ground floor.

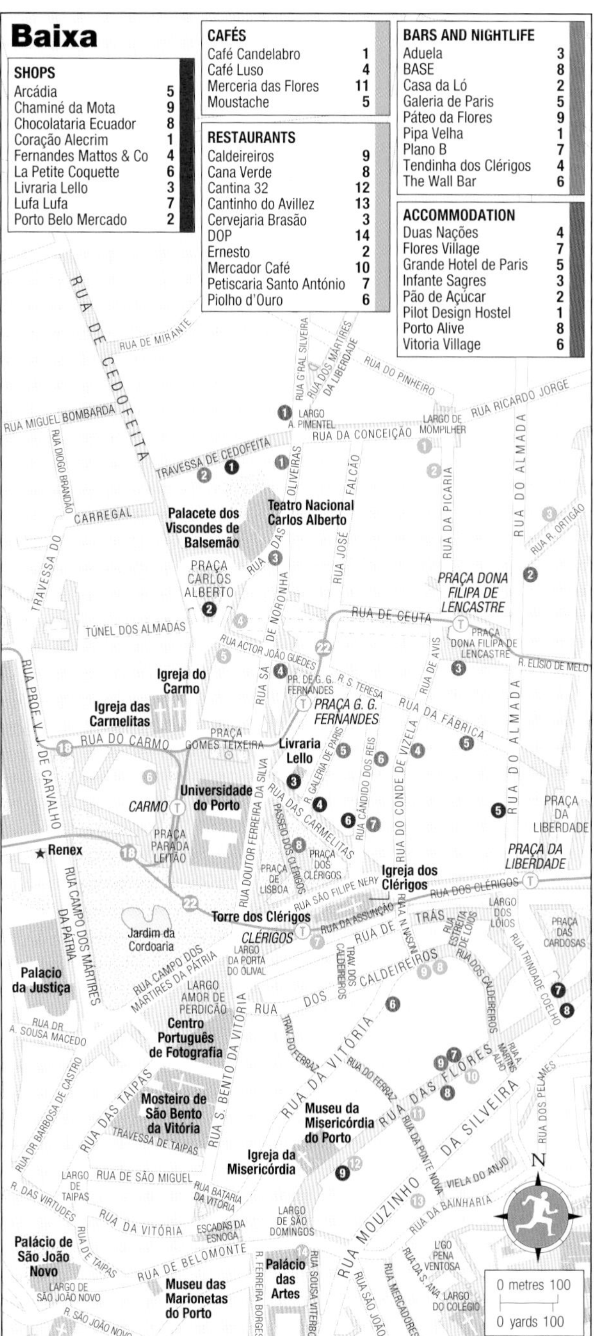
Baixa
SHOPS
Arcádia 5
Chaminé da Mota 9
Chocolataria Ecuador 8
Coração Alecrim 1
Fernandes Mattos & Co 4
La Petite Coquette 6
Livraria Lello 3
Lufa Lufa 7
Porto Belo Mercado 2
CAFÉS
Café Candelabro 1
Café Luso 4
Merceria das Flores 11
Moustache 5
RESTAURANTS
Caldeireiros 9
Cana Verde 8
Cantina 32 12
Cantinho do Avillez 13
Cervejaria Brasão 3
DOP 14
Ernesto 2
Mercador Café 10
Petiscaria Santo António 7
Piolho d'Ouro 6
BARS AND NIGHTLIFE
Aduela 3
BASE 8
Casa da Ló 2
Galeria de Paris 5
Páteo da Flores 9
Pipa Velha 1
Plano B 7
Tendinha dos Clérigos 4
The Wall Bar 6
ACCOMMODATION
Duas Nações 4
Flores Village 7
Grande Hotel de Paris 5
Infante Sagres 3
Pão de Açúcar 2
Pilot Design Hostel 1
Porto Alive 8
Vitoria Village 6
RUA DE CEDOFEITA
RUA DE MIRANTE
RUA G'RAL SILVEIRA
RUA DOS MÁRTIRES DA LIBERDADE
RUA DO PINHEIRO
RUA RICARDO JORGE
RUA MIGUEL BOMBARDA
LARGO A. PIMENTEL
RUA DA CONCEIÇÃO
LARGO DE MOMPILHER
RUA DIOGO BRANDÃO
TRAVESSA DE CEDOFEITA
CARREGAL
Palacete dos Viscondes de Balsemão
Teatro Nacional Carlos Alberto
RUA DAS OLIVEIRAS
RUA JOSÉ FALCÃO
RUA DA PICARIA
RUA DO ALMADA
RUA R. ORTIGÃO
TRAVESSA DO CARREGAL
PRAÇA CARLOS ALBERTO
RUA DE NORONHA
PRAÇA DONA FILIPA DE LENCASTRE
RUA DE CEUTA
TÚNEL DOS ALMADAS
RUA ACTOR JOÃO GUEDES
R. ELISIO DE MELO
Igreja do Carmo
RUA SÁ
PR. DE G. G. FERNANDES
R. S. TERESA
RUA DE AVIS
Igreja das Carmelitas
PRAÇA G. G. FERNANDES
RUA DA FÁBRICA
RUA PROF. V. J. DE CARVALHO
RUA DO CARMO
PRAÇA GOMES TEIXEIRA
Livraria Lello
R. GALERIA DE PARIS
RUA CÂNDIDO DOS REIS
RUA DO CONDE DE VIZELA
Universidade do Porto
CARMO
RUA DAS CARMELITAS
PASSEIO DOS CLÉRIGOS
PRAÇA DA LIBERDADE
PRAÇA PARADA LEITÃO
RUA DOUTOR FERREIRA DA SILVA
Renex
PRAÇA DOS CLÉRIGOS
PRAÇA DE LISBOA
Igreja dos Clérigos
RUA SÃO FILIPE NERY
RUA DOS CLÉRIGOS
RUA CAMPO DOS MÁRTIRES DA PÁTRIA
Torre dos Clérigos
RUA DA ASSUNÇÃO
RUA DE TRÁS
LARGO DOS LÓIOS
PRAÇA DAS CARDOSAS
Jardim da Cordoaria
CLÉRIGOS
LARGO DA PORTA DO OLIVAL
TRAV. DOS CALDEIREIROS
RUA DOS CALDEIREIROS
RUA TRINDADE COELHO
Palacio da Justiça
LARGO AMOR DE PERDIÇÃO
RUA DR. A. SOUSA MACEDO
Centro Português de Fotografia
RUA DA VITÓRIA
TRAV. DO FERRAZ
RUA DO FERRAZ
RUA DAS FLORES
RUA DOS PELAMES
RUA DR BARBOSA DE CASTRO
RUA DAS TAIPAS
Mosteiro de São Bento da Vitória
RUA S. BENTO DA VITÓRIA
Museu da Misericórdia do Porto
RUA DA PONTE NOVA
RUA DA SILVEIRA
TRAVESSA DE TAIPAS
Igreja da Misericórdia
LARGO DE TAIPAS
RUA DE SÃO MIGUEL
RUA BATARIA DA VITÓRIA
VIELA DO ANJO
R. DAS VIRTUDES
RUA DA VITÓRIA
LARGO DE SÃO DOMINGOS
RUA MOUZINHO DA SILVEIRA
RUA DA BAINHARIA
ESCADAS DA ESNOGA
Palácio de São João Novo
RUA DE TAIPAS
RUA DE BELOMONTE
L'GO PENA VENTOSA
LARGO DE SÃO JOÃO NOVO
Museu das Marionetas do Porto
R. FERREIRA BORGES
Palácio das Artes
RUA SOUSA VITERBO
RUA SÃO JOÃO
RUA DOS MERCADORES
RUA DAS S. ANA
LARGO DO COLÉGIO
R. SÃO JOÃO NOVO
N
0 metres 100
0 yards 100

Igreja dos Clérigos

Rua das Flores

With its grand wrought-iron balconied buildings and tiled facades, the attractive street of **Rua das Flores** dates back to the sixteenth century when it was laid out on land belonging to Porto's bishop, and named after the existing orchards and gardens. In the nineteenth century, Rua das Flores became Porto's upmarket shopping street, with wealthy traders such as goldsmiths colonizing the northern side and other trades, like fabric sellers, setting up shop on the south side. However, the street later suffered a decline, and many of its buildings fell into disrepair and were abandoned. Over the last decade, a large-scale regeneration project has seen the street pedestrianized and its beautiful buildings renovated and restored to their former grandeur. New shops, cafés and restaurants have opened up and, today, the street is a real pleasure to stroll down, browsing around the artisan food and craft shops, admiring the colourful tiled facades and lingering for a coffee at one of its many pavement cafés.

Torre dos Clérigos and Igreja dos Clérigos

MAP p.49, POCKET MAP D5
Rua São Filipe Nery ⓦ torredosclerigos.pt. Daily 9am–7pm, last entry 6.30pm. €4.

The best vantage point in the city centre is from the top of the Baroque **Torre dos Clérigos**, which towers 75m above the city streets. This slender finger-like structure was the tallest building in Portugal when it was built in 1763 and, once you've puffed your way up the two hundred-odd stairs, you can enjoy sweeping views from the top. Before you leave, step through the door into the associated church, the **Igreja dos Clérigos** – designed, like the tower, by busy Porto architect Nicolau Nasoni (see box, opposite), who, after half a lifetime spent in his adopted city, was buried in the church at his own request.

Jardim da Cordoaria

MAP p.49, POCKET MAP C5–D5

The main university building in Porto flanks one side of the **Jardim da Cordoaria**, the "Garden of rope-makers", which was named after the rope-makers who once worked here. It's a lovely space, with gigantic plane trees sheltering huddles of students and old men playing impromptu card and chess games. Look out for the statue called *Thirteen People Laughing at Each Other*, by Spanish sculptor Juan Muñoz, which dates from 2001 when Porto was named the European Capital of Culture. There are more monumental buildings on all sides, and a clutch of alluring pavement cafés flanking Praça de Parada Leitão. Two of Porto's trams leave from alongside the gardens, the circular route #22 to Batalha and #18 which runs to the Palácio de Cristal (see p.76).

Centro Português de Fotografia

MAP p.49, POCKET MAP D6
Largo Amor de Perdiçâo ⓣ 220 046 300, ⓦ www.cpf.pt. March–June & Sept–Oct Tues–Fri 10am–6pm, Sat, Sun & hols 3–7pm; July–Aug daily 10am–6pm; Nov–Feb Tues–Fri 10am–12.30pm & 2–5pm, Sat, Sun & hols 3–7pm. Free.

The imposing Neoclassical building to the south of the Jardim da Cordoaria – distinguished by 103, mostly barred, windows – was the city's eighteenth-century prison, the Cadeia da Relação. The prison remained in use until the revolution of 1974 but it is now the headquarters of the **Centro Português de Fotografia**, which has restored the building's cells, chambers, workshops and internal courtyards and converted them into rather extraordinary exhibition spaces. Temporary shows cover anything from vintage Portuguese photography to contemporary urban work from Brazil and elsewhere.

On the museum's top floor there is a collection of antique cameras and photographic equipment, ranging from the "stereo-graphoscope" of 1885 to all manner of classic Kodaks and Yashicas. The museum is impressive, though it's the history of the building itself which holds much of the interest. It was built in 1767 in a wedge shape to fit between the old city walls and a convent, and the prisoners were allocated cells according to the severity of their crimes, their status and their ability to pay. The worst offenders were put in damp dungeons accessed by a trap door from above; women were kept in communal cells on the second floor, while on the top floor there were the "Malta Rooms" – airy individual cells with views over the city, where "people of status" were only locked in at night. The huge prison also had its own infirmary, guards' living quarters and a courthouse.

Porto's historic architecture

Porto's churches provide one of the country's richest concentrations of **Baroque** architecture. The style was brought to Portugal by Italian painter and architect **Nicolau Nasoni** (1691–1773), who arrived in Porto at the age of 34, and remained there for the rest of his life. The church and tower of Clérigos is his greatest work, though his masterful touch can also be seen in the Sé cathedral and adjacent bishop's palace, and at the churches of Misericórdia, Carmo, Santo Ildefonso and São Francisco. All are remarkable for their decorative exuberance, reflecting the wealth derived from Portugal's colonies.

In the second half of the eighteenth century, out went the luxuriant complexity of Baroque and in came the studied lines of the **Neoclassical** period. Neoclassicism also incorporated hints of Gothic and Baroque art, but most of all, was influenced by Islamic style, which reached its apotheosis in the Salão Árabe of the Palácio da Bolsa. By the turn of the twentieth century Porto's Neoclassicism had acquired a French **Renaissance** touch, thanks largely to the architect **José Marquês da Silva** (1869–1947), who studied in Paris. His most notable works were São Bento station, the exuberant Teatro Nacional São João, and the distinctly less elegant monument to the Peninsular War that dominates the Rotunda da Boavista.

Igreja do Carmo

MAP p.49, POCKET MAP D4
Rua do Carmo ⓣ 223 322 928. Daily 8.30am–6.30pm. Free.

Beyond the north side of the Jardim da Cordoaria, across from the university, the eighteenth-century **Igreja do Carmo** has two instantly recognizable traits – its deliriously over-the-top exterior *azulejos* and the four saints atop the facade, seemingly poised to jump. Inside, the elegant gilt carvings are among the finest examples of Portuguese Rococo.

Igreja das Carmelitas

MAP p.49, POCKET MAP C4–D4
Rua do Carmo ⓣ 222 050 279. Mon–Fri 7.30am–7pm, Sat & Sun 9am–6.45pm. Free.

The older and rather more sober **Igreja das Carmelitas** lies almost – but not quite – adjacent to the Igrejo do Carmo because of a law that stipulated that no two churches were to share the same wall (in this case perhaps to hinder amorous liaisons between the nuns of Carmelitas and the monks of Carmo). As a result, what is probably the narrowest house in Portugal – barely 1m wide, and with its own letterbox – was built between them and, though now empty, remained inhabited until the 1980s.

Igreja do Carmo

Livraria Lello

MAP p.49, POCKET MAP D5
Rua das Carmelitas 144 ⓣ 222 002 037, ⓦ livrarialello.pt. Mon–Fri 10am–7.30pm, Sat 10am–7pm. Ticket office two doors down the street at Armazéns do Castelo, at Rua das Carmelitas 166. €4 entry redeemable against any purchase.

Porto's famous galleried Art Nouveau **bookshop**, with its Neo-Gothic exterior and inner staircase just begging for a grand entrance, is a delight beyond words. It was founded by the well-to-do Lello brothers and intellectuals in 1906 and specialized in limited edition books – many of which are still here (see p.55). The brothers now appear as bas-reliefs on the walls, alongside busts of great writers including Eça de Queiroz and Cervantes. The Lellos commissioned an engineer and fellow bibliophile Francisco Xavier Esteves to design the interior, which is simply stunning. The ground floor even has rails set into the floor for transporting book "carriages". The impressive double, freestanding staircase (actually made of concrete) lures people upstairs where you can admire the extraordinary plasterwork ceiling, which resembles ornately carved wood. Columns and a stained-glass roof light add to the air of something far grander than a simple bookshop, the whole design having an almost organic feel, as if the walls and ceiling are the ribs and bones of a living creature. The first floor was the traditional meeting point of artists and intellectuals, and was frequented by J K Rowling during her time in Porto in the 1990s (see box, opposite). It is this, and the similarity of the shop's decor to some of Hogwarts' more outlandish design characteristics, that has put the bookshop firmly on the tourist circuit, with up to four thousand people visiting daily. There are often queues to get in, but if you come first thing in the morning or in the evening shortly before closing time, you may be able to experience the place more as a bookshop than a tourist site.

Praça de Lisboa

MAP p.49, POCKET MAP D5

The broad **Praça de Lisboa** is one of Porto's most fashionable squares. In the middle of it, you'll find the Passeio dos Clérigos, a mini shopping mall beneath a concrete mantel, all neatly landscaped on top with lawns and gnarled olive trees. Just off the square, Rua Cândido dos Reis is lined with handsome Art Nouveau buildings, laid out in the early nineteenth century after the demolition of an old convent. It's now the hub of Porto's nightlife scene, lined with clubs and bars, and also hosts a crafts market on the second and last Saturday of the month.

Palacete dos Viscondes de Balsemão

MAP p.49, POCKET MAP D4
Praça Carlos Alberta 71 ⓣ 223 393 480. Mon–Fri 9am–8pm, Sat 10am–1pm & 2–7pm. Free.

Built in the nineteenth century for the wealthy Godinho family, and briefly home to the exiled King of Sardinia, this small **palace** now houses an exhibition centre in two of its rooms. One hosts temporary exhibits, the other an interesting collection of historic coins, including some dating back to the birth of the country. Adjacent to the palace, a separate exhibition space, The Bank of Materials, displays important materials salvaged by the town council from historic buildings. There's a range of beautiful *azulejos* dating from the fifteenth century, mostly taken from building facades, along with a collection of historic street signs and roof tiles – it's certainly worth a browse on a wet day.

J K Rowling's spell in Porto

J K Rowling moved to Porto to teach English in 1991, and it was here that she started writing the *Harry Potter* novels. She married a local journalist, Jorge Arantes, and moved into his mother's apartment in Rua do Duque de Saldanha. They had a daughter in 1993, but separated the same year. Arantes later claimed he had helped come up with ideas for the Harry Potter novels, which have earned Rowling more than £600 million – though she denies this. Rowling subsequently returned to Edinburgh with her daughter and the first three chapters of her Harry Potter novel. Her life in Portugal clearly influenced aspects of the books: one of Hogwarts' founding professors was Salazar Slytherin (Salazar being Portugal's notorious dictator for much of the twentieth century), while many of Potter's spells can be easily understood by Portuguese speakers: witness *aguamenti* (bring out water), *duro* (make things hard), *protego* (protect people) and *silencio* (to silence people). There are many similarities, too, between Porto's more characterful buildings and elements of Hogwarts, notably the fantastical decor of the Livraria Lello bookshop (see opposite), with its twisting double staircase – though Rowling has always refused to confirm or deny its influence.

Shops

Arcádia

MAP p.49, POCKET MAP E5
Rua do Almada 63 ⓣ 222 001 518, ⓦ arcadia.pt. Mon–Fri 9.30am–7pm, Sat 9.30am–1pm.

The Bastos family has been making chocolates in Porto since 1933 using top-quality natural ingredients. There are several branches around the city now (including one at Rua de Santa Catarina 191), but this is the original with its blue-tiled walls and wooden interior. The chocolates are delicious and come in a variety of flavours including cinnamon and ginger, tangerine and, of course, port.

Chaminé da Mota

MAP p.49, POCKET MAP D6
Rua das Flores 28 ⓣ 222 005 380. Mon–Fri 9am–12.30pm & 2.30–7pm.

Founded in 1981, this bookshop is an Aladdin's cave of old books and objects, including rare tomes, magazines, ancient radios and record-players, posters and even a mini printing press. You may not necessarily want to buy anything, but it's a fascinating place to wander around and listen to the giant music boxes that play when you put €2 in.

Chocolataria Ecuador

MAP p.49, POCKET MAP E5
Rua das Flores 298 ⓣ 222 018 167. Daily 11am–2pm & 2.30–7.30pm.

This tiny shop sells the city's best chocolate, with a top-quality selection of artisan chocolates sold by weight – they come in a variety of flavours, including praline and Jamaican pepper, and mango. The blocks of chocolate are sublime too – try the dark chocolate with curry or dark chocolate with port. There's a second (larger) branch at Rua Sá da Bandeira 637.

Arcádia

Coração Alecrim

MAP p.49, POCKET MAP D3
Trav de Cedofeita 28 ⓣ 938 111 152. Mon–Sat 11am–7pm.

Lovely shop selling local handmade textiles, clothes, jewellery, ceramics and plants, as well as eco-friendly and sustainable vintage-style and designer clothing and homeware.

Fernandes Mattos & Co

MAP p.49, POCKET MAP D5
Rua dos Carmelitas 108–114 ⓣ 222 005 568. Mon–Sat 10am–8pm, Sun 11am–7pm.

On the ground floor of a lovely old building, this shop started life in 1886 as a fabric store. It still has the traditional wooden floors, shelves and cabinets, but today it sells all kinds of retro and vintage-style artefacts, such as posters, games, toys and biscuit tins, as well as more contemporary mugs and rucksacks. Upstairs on the first floor, a branch of A Vida Portuguesa sells traditional ceramics, textiles and soaps.

La Petite Coquette

MAP p.49, POCKET MAP D5
Rua Cândido dos Reis 25 ⓣ 916 802 033. Mon–Sat 11am–7pm.

Press the bell and climb the stairs to enter a treasure trove of secondhand designer labels, including Gucci bags, bling Chanel trainers, shoes by Yves Saint-Laurent and dresses by Missoni and Valentino. Prices vary according to the condition of the goods, but everything here is a bargain – if you're lucky, you may pick up a Gucci blouse for €65, a pair of Jimmy Choos for €125, or an immaculate barely worn Victoria Beckham dress for €465.

Livraria Lello

MAP p.49, POCKET MAP D5
Rua das Carmelitas 144 ⓣ 222 002 037. Mon–Fri 10am–7.30pm, Sat 10am–7pm.

Porto's famous galleried Art Nouveau shop has become a tourist sight in its own right (see p.52), but behind the crowds this still remains one of the citys best bookshops. There's general fiction on the ground floor (including, of course, the Harry Potter stories in many different languages), much of it in English, with reference and non-fiction (including travel) on the upper floor. You can also find rare editions of Portuguese books. Look out, too, for the original till, made in 1881, the first in Portugal to issue paper receipts and with prices in reis (the currency before the escudo). You'll get your €4 entry fee back on any purchase.

Lufa Lufa

MAP p.49, POCKET MAP E5
Rua das Flores 191. Daily 11am–2pm & 3–5pm.

Small shop specializing in organic, locally designed cotton T-shirts, with innovative Porto-themed logos (for example, Porto written to resemble a bicycle). T-shirts from around €15.

Porto Belo Mercado

MAP p.49, POCKET MAP D4
Praça Carlos Alberto. Sat 10am–7pm.

This small market has stall-holders selling everything from LPs and old toys to handicrafts and home-made food. Its name, meaning beautiful Porto, is a nod to London's well-known, and considerably larger, market.

Livraria Lello

Cafés

Café Candelabro

MAP p.49, POCKET MAP E3
Rua da Conceição 3. Mon–Fri 10am–2am, Sat 4pm–2am, Sun 4pm–midnight.

This is a very popular café-bar and bookshop full of old typewriters and photography and art books, which you can purchase or read at the tables. Not surprisingly it attracts an arty crowd and morphs into a hip bar in the evenings. Your food options are limited to snacks and nibbles (sandwiches cost around €4), but it serves a mean gin 'n' tonic and chilled glass of *vinho verde*.

Café Luso

MAP p.49, POCKET MAP D4
Praça Carlos Alberto 92 ⓣ 224 154 293. Daily 11am–midnight.

This long-established café featuring wooden floors and dating back to 1935 is in a good location with tables and chairs outside on the square. *Café Luso* serves the usual Porto café staples, such as *francesinhos* (€9), omelettes (€7) and *pregos* (€5). You can also have more substantial dishes including roast goat (€15).

Merceria das Flores

MAP p.49, POCKET MAP E6
Rua das Flores 110 ⓣ 222 083 232, ⓦ mercearіadasflores.com. Mon–Thurs 10.30am–9pm, Fri & Sat 10.30am–10pm, Sun 1–8pm.

This lovely little deli/café sells regional and organic produce, including tinned fish of all descriptions, olive oils and wines. It's a great place to browse or you can settle down at the tables in the pedestrianized street in front for a coffee and cake, or for lunch – try the toasted sandwich of local sheep's cheese, with honey and almond (€5), or opt for a platter of regional cheese and meats (€10).

Moustache

MAP p.49, POCKET MAP D4
Praça Carlos Alberta 104 ⓣ 222 082 916. Mon 10am–8pm, Tues & Wed 10am–midnight, Thurs–Sat 10am–2am, Sun 2–8pm.

Simple but bustling café serving a good range of inexpensive smoothies, innovative frappés, sumptuous cakes – a slice of Ferrero Roche cheesecake anyone? – and quiches in an attractive balconied building with seats on the square. Cakes start at around €2.50 a slice, and frappés from €3. It's more of a bar in the evening, when it attracts a young crowd.

Merceria das FLores

Restaurants

Caldeireiros

MAP p.49, POCKET MAP E5
Rua dos Caldeireiros 139 ⓣ 223 214 074. Mon–Sat noon–3pm & 5.30pm–1am.

With stylish but simple decor – the plain painted walls are dotted with colourful tiles and mini-chandeliers hang from the ceiling – this long, thin restaurant has communal bench tables and serves tasty and reasonably priced food. The menu features a selection of tapas (€4–6), plus main courses such as *filletes de pescada* (€9) or a Mirandese steak (€12.50). They also do a half *francesinho* for €5 – a good idea if you want to sample this hearty Porto speciality without feeling completely stuffed afterwards.

Cana Verde

MAP p.49, POCKET MAP E5
Rua dos Caldeireiros 121 ⓣ 222 018 042. Mon–Fri noon–3.30pm.

Locals queue outside this tiny restaurant with its blue-tiled walls and few tables on the street for the cheap and cheerful, filling lunchtime dishes. Large, good-value plates of traditional dishes such as *filletes de pescada*, grilled chicken or *febras* are all accompanied by tasty tomato rice and cost €5–6. Meanwhile the set lunch is a steal, with soup, bread, dish-of-the-day and a coffee for €7.

Cantina 32

MAP p.49, POCKET MAP D6
Rua das Flores 32 ⓣ 222 039 069. Mon–Thurs 12.30–3pm & 6.30–10.30pm, Fri & Sat 12.30–3pm & 6.30–11pm.

With its industrial-style interior, long bench tables and seating outside on the street in front, this is a good spot for a quick snack and a drink or to linger for a full meal. The *petiscos* (€7–8 a dish) are tasty – try the *bacalhau*, or carpaccio with truffle sauce – while main courses such as squid and shrimp stew or tiger prawns with garlic butter start at €11.50. Don't miss the delicious banana cheesecake served in a flower pot, with crumbled Oreo "soil" on top.

Cantinho do Avillez

MAP p.49, POCKET MAP E6
Rua Mouzinha da Silveira 166 ⓣ 223 227 879, ⓦ cantinhodoavillez.pt/en. Mon–Fri 12.30–3pm & 7pm–midnight, Sat & Sun 12.30pm–midnight.

Michelin-Star chef José Avillez' first Porto outlet, *Cantinho do Avillez* is an excellent place to sample top-quality and inventive Portuguese food at surprisingly affordable prices – most mains are around €18. This welcoming restaurant with a tiled floor and retro-style decor may be laid-back and informal, but the food is innovative and interesting, with Avillez' unusual takes on Portuguese classics – sample the likes of lightly cooked tuna, scallops, game sausage and his famous burgers, not to mention the signature exploding olives. Leave room for the delicious desserts, too, such as fruit salad with mojito foam.

Cervejaria Brasão

MAP p.49, POCKET MAP E3
Rua de Ramalho Ortigão 28 ⓣ 934 158 672. Mon–Wed & Sun noon–3pm & 7pm–midnight, Fri–Sat noon–3pm & 7pm–2am.

This modern take on an old-fashioned *cervejaria* (beer hall), is hugely popular. As well as decent beer, you'll find a range of snacky food including *pregos* (steak sandwiches), various *francesinhos* (around €7) and *petiscos* (from €4). There are also mains including sumptuous steaks (€17).

DOP

MAP p.49, POCKET MAP D6
Palácio das Artes, Largo São Domingos 18

DOP

ⓣ 222 014 313, ⓦ ruipaula.com. Mon 7.30–11pm, Tues–Sat 12.30–3pm & 7.30–11pm.

Come here to see well-known Porto chef Rui Paula wow punters with the creative Portuguese cuisine that made his name (see box, p.79). These sleek downtown premises are "a place to taste and be bold" – so expect a twist on traditional cuisine, with dishes like suckling pig in a cider sauce or lamb couscous with aubergine ravioli (mains from €26). Tasting menus cost €80, with wine pairings for another €30. You should be able to rock up for lunch, but in the evenings dinner reservations are advised.

Ernesto

MAP p.49, POCKET MAP E3
Rua da Picaria 85 ⓣ 222 002 600. Mon 11.30am–3pm, Tues–Fri 11.30am–3.30pm & 6.30–9.30pm, Sat 11.30am–3.30pm & 6.30–11pm.

A pleasantly old-fashioned restaurant dating back to the 1930s which proudly displays an autographed menu from Bono of U2. The regional food is excellent, with the menu usually featuring the likes of roast goat, veal, octopus and *bacalhau*, along with the fresh fish of the day. Prices for the main dishes start at €14.

BASE

Mercador Café

MAP p.49, POCKET MAP 56
Rua das Flores 180 ⓣ 223 323 041. Mon–Sat 8.30am–8pm.

Lovely high-ceilinged café in an old fabric store with the original wooden cabinets inside and tables on the street in front. It serves pastries, coffees and lunch, as well as more substantial dishes such as pork with asparagus and port sauce (€13.50). There's usually also a dish-of-the-day or two (€8–9), which changes regularly, but may well feature the likes of cod and onions, or mushroom risotto with duck.

Petiscaria Santo António

MAP p.49, POCKET MAP D5
Rua da Assunção 40 ⓣ 938 704 632. Tues–Thurs noon–midnight, Fri & Sat 12.30pm–1am.

This tiny place with wooden tables has a cosy atmosphere and serves up delicious dishes made from Portuguese and local ingredients where possible – try the tasty goat's cheese with smoked ham, honey and raisins (€6), the tinned sardine salad (€5) or the *chouriço assado*, which is served flaming at the table (€6).

Piolho d'Ouro

MAP p.49, POCKET MAP C5
Praça Parada Leitão 43–55 ⓣ 222 003 749. Mon–Sat 7am–late.

Since 1909, this no-frills traditional café-restaurant has been serving students from the nearby university with large, cheap plates of food. Always busy, it has dark wooden furniture, football on the TV most nights and tables out on the square in front. Good for a coffee or drink, they also do soups, salads and sandwiches from €3, omelettes from €6, plus large portions of *pescada* with Russian salad or *febras* with chips for €6.

Bars and clubs

Aduela

MAP p.49, POCKET MAP D4
Rua das Oliveiras 36 ⓣ 222 084 398. Mon 3pm–2am, Tues–Thurs noon–2am, Fri & Sat noon–4am, Sun 3pm–midnight.

A traditional bar which is now very on trend, with outdoor seating beneath a gnarled olive tree. There's a good range of wines, mojitos and sangria, as well as inexpensive snacks.

BASE

MAP p.49, POCKET MAP D5
Jardim dos Clérigos, Praça de Lisboa ⓣ 910 076 920. Daily: late March–April & Sept–Oct 10am–8pm; May–Aug 10am–2am.

Perched on the grassed-over concrete top of the Passeio dos Clérigos shopping mall, this is a hip café-bar serving hot and cold drinks, including a fine range of cocktails. Take a seat at the wooden benches beneath the umbrellas, surrounded by olive trees. It also serves sandwiches (from €6) and snacks.

Casa da Ló

MAP p.49, POCKET MAP D3
Tv do Cedofeita 20a ⓣ 220 119 738. Mon–Wed 3pm–midnight, Thurs–Sat 3pm–4am.

A rustic-chic former bakery with

an old marble bar, two rooms with wooden tables and a small courtyard at the back. It's a great place to chill out over a drink, with regular DJ sets at weekends.

Galeria de Paris

MAP p.49, POCKET MAP D4
Rua Galeria de Paris 36 ⓣ 222 016 218. Daily 8.30am–3am.

This bar-café with ceiling fans has an eclectic collection of things hanging on its walls, including a Fiat car, guitars, dolls and even a toilet. It's a quirky, fun place, with live music in the evenings ranging from fado to pop, and belly-dancing performances. The food is good, with fish dishes, steak and pork chops (from €9.50) and some veggie options too.

Páteo da Flores

MAP p.49, POCKET MAP E6
Rua das Flores 135 ⓣ 222 031 128. Mon 7.30–11pm, Tues–Sat 12.30pm–11pm.

This friendly wine/tapas bar may look small from the street, but it opens out onto a lovely tiled patio at the back, covered with a dramatic glass roof. It's a great place to sample some of the wines on their extensive list accompanied by a selection of tapas (€4–10), such as tasty padron peppers, or a sharing board of smoked hams and cheese (€17).

Pipa Velha

MAP p.49, POCKET MAP D3
Rua das Oliveiras 75 ⓣ 223 222 780. Daily 6pm–4am.

Long-established, laidback bar with old theatre posters on the walls. It's a good spot for drinks, as well as inexpensive *petiscos*, including a fine flaming *choriço*.

Plano B

MAP p.49, POCKET MAP D5
Rua Cândido dos Reis 30 ⓣ 222 012 500, ⓦ planobporto.com. Tues & Wed 10pm–2am, Thurs 10pm–4am, Fri & Sat 10pm–6am.

Swanky, fashionable and spacious club, with two dance floors, regular local and international DJ sessions and occasional live music, too. There's an upstairs bar for when things get too frenetic downstairs, and a rather grand Greek-style statue by the downstairs bar. On Friday and Saturday nights, there may be an entrance fee of €5–10 depending on who's playing.

Tendinha dos Clérigos

MAP p.49, POCKET MAP E4
Rua Conde Vizela 80 ⓣ 222 011 438, ⓦ tendinhadosclerigos.com. Wed–Sat midnight–6am.

One for rockers – a cave-like bar and club with pool table and dance floor, that's also a regular venue for DJs and up-and-coming bands. This is where people come after the other bars have closed, so best to get here before 4am unless you like it truly frenetic. Friday and Saturday nights there's a minimum consumption of €6.

The Wall Bar

MAP p.49, POCKET MAP D4
Rua Cândido dos Reis 90 ⓣ 222 086 557. Mon–Sat 5pm–4am, Sun 9pm–4am.

One of the hippest nightspots on the fashionable Rua Cândido dos Reis – its name comes from the wacky wall of drinks behind the bar on one side and a map of the world made up of country names on the other. It doesn't get going much before midnight, after which it can be packed. Expect good sounds and a fine range of cocktails.

Plano B

Vila Nova de Gaia

Though Porto lent its name to port, it's Vila Nova de Gaia, on the opposite bank of the Douro, which is the birthplace of the city's famous drink. Here, a succession of port wine lodges grew up in the twelfth century because of the suitably humid conditions – and they continue to dominate the steep slopes of the southern riverfront today. No visit to the city is complete without a tour or tasting at a historic lodge, although Gaia also has plenty of other attractions. Its waterfront cable car offers fantastic views over historic Porto, with even better vistas from the hilltop Mosteiro de Serra do Pilar. Harder to reach, but worth seeking out are the engaging house museum, Casa-Museu Teixeira Lopes, and the city's main zoo, Santo Inácio.

The riverfront

Facing Porto's Ribeira, Vila Nova de Gaia's pretty **riverfront** is a real pleasure to stroll along – with its long line of cafés, bars and restaurants, and wooden artisan stalls selling souvenirs. The cable car glides silently overhead, cruise boats dock alongside the esplanade, while the wooden boats with sails, known as *barcos rabelos*, moor out in the river: cormorants dry themselves on the rudders of these traditional boats, which were once used to transport wine casks downriver from the Douro port estates. The views are, if anything, better from Vila Nova de Gaia than from the Porto side, as they look back across to a largely eighteenth-century cityscape, with few modern buildings intruding in on the panoramic sweep from the Palácio de Cristal gardens in

Vila Nova de Gaia's riverfront

Getting to Vila Nova de Gaia

There are various ways of getting over the river to Vila Nova de Gaia, depending on where you are starting from. If you are on the Ribeira riverfront, you can simply **walk** over the lower level of the Ponte de Dom Luís I – a ten-minute walk with the bonus of good views en route. Alternatively, you can take the Douro **river taxi**, which takes five minutes to shuttle across the river from the Cais de Estiva to Gaia's riverfront (daily 10am–sunset every 15 minutes or so; €3; douroriverstaxi.com). If you're in Porto's upper town, you can take **buses** #900, #90 1 and #906 from São Bento station across the bridge and along the Gaia riverfront. Alternatively, you can either walk across the upper level of the bridge to the Jardim de Morro, or take **metro** Line D from Aliados/São Bento to Jardim do Morro; from here you can take the Teleférico de Gaia or walk down to the riverfront.

the west, the Ribeira district and Torre de Cleigos straight ahead and the cathedral towers and Ponte de Dom Luís I to the east.

Teleférico de Gaia

MAP p.62, POCKET MAP D9
Lower station at Cais de Gaia, upper station at Jardim do Morro 223 741 440, gaiacablecar.com. Daily: late March to late April & late Sept to late Oct 10am–7pm; late April to late Sept 10am–8pm; late Oct to late March 10am–6pm. €6 one-way, €9 return; children half-price.

A good way to explore Gaia – and to take some dramatic aerial shots of Porto and the river – is to ride the **Teleférico de Gaia**, or cable car. Connecting the upper station at the Jardim de Morro, near the top level of the Ponte de Dom Luís I, with the far end of the Gaia riverside, the five-minute, 600m journey sweeps right above the rooftops of Vila Nova de Gaia's historic port wine lodges.

Mosteiro de Serra do Pilar

MAP p.62, POCKET MAP F9–G9
Largo de Avis 220 142 425. Tues–Sun 10am–5.30pm. €2, or €4 including the dome.

Spread along the hilltop above Vila Nova de Gaia, the **Moistero de Serra do Pilar** is remarkable for its circular design. Originally modelled on Rome's church of Santa Maria de Redondo, it is the only church in Portugal to have a circular vault and cloisters. The Moistero de Serra de Pilar was built in the sixteenth century for the Order of St Augustine, but its construction lasted over 70 years, during which time Portugal was taken over by the Spanish – hence the monastery being named after a Spanish saint. The monastery was requisitioned by the military during the nineteenth century, with first Wellington, then Napoleon billeting their troops at its defensive heights.

Today protected by UNESCO Heritage status, the church offers fantastic views over the river and city from the terrace outside. However, those with a head for heights can get an even more impressive view by taking a tour (approximately hourly; except Sunday morning) up the dome. On the tour, guides lead you up the 104 steps to walk around a narrow balcony that runs around the outside of the dome: all the tours are escorted by a soldier, since the monastery still belongs to the military.

Jardim do Morro

Next to cable car's upper exit, and accessible from central Porto by walking over the top tier of the Ponte de Dom Luís I or taking the metro to **Jardim do Morro**, these small gardens sit on a hillock above the river, with great views back over town. The lawns and shady palms make this a relaxing place to hang out and a popular spot to watch the sun rise.

Igreja de Santa Marinha

MAP p.62

Largo Santa Marinha. No set opening times.

This is one of Vila Nova de Gaia's oldest churches, remodelled in the seventeenth century by Nicolau Nasoni (see box, p.51) on the site of a fifteenth-century temple. There are beautiful *azulejos* above the alter and the usual Baroque flourishes, though the church is often kept locked.

Zoo Santo Inácio

MAP p.62

Rua 5 de Outubro 4503, Avintes ⊕ 227 878 500, ⓦ zoosantoinacio.com. April–Sept daily 10am–7pm; Oct–Dec, Feb & March Tues–Sun 10am–5pm. €13.50, 3–12 year-olds €9.50, under-2s free.

This small, well-run **zoo** houses some eight hundred animals, including lions, giraffes, water buffaloes and Siberian tigers. All the animals here are living in spaces designed to be as close to their natural habitat as possible. The zoo houses many endangered species, including the snow leopard, and has an active breeding programme to try and improve the numbers of vulnerable species. Throughout the day there are various demonstrations and feeding sessions but the highlight is the glass walk-through tunnel in the Asian lions' cage.

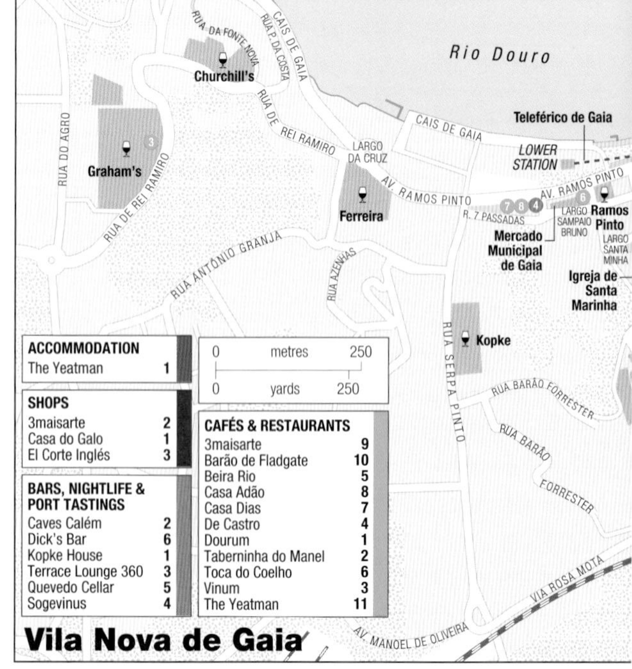

Casa-Museu Teixeira Lopes

MAP p.62

Rua de Teixeira Lopes 32 ⓣ 351 223 751 224, Ⓜ Camara de Gaia. Tues–Fri 9am–12.30pm & 2–5pm, Sat 9am–noon & 2–5pm, Sun 10am–noon & 2–5pm. Free.

The **Casa-Museu Teixeira Lopes** is interesting on two levels – first for its large collection of works by sculptor António Teixeira Lopes (1866–1942) and secondly for its insight into life in a wealthy late-nineteenth-century house. The house was built in 1895 by Teixeira Lopes' brother, architect José Teixeira Lopes, as a residence and studio, and has been restored to its former condition. You enter through a pretty garden dotted with sculptures and trees and with views over to the city, then pass through a series of restored rooms including Teixeira's bedroom, office and dining room, all furnished with the sculptor's personal effects and family paintings. A balconied gallery looks down onto Teixeira's vast well-lit studio, while a connecting door leads through to the Diogo de Macedo galleries. These contain works by Diogo de Macedo (1889–1959), a student of Teixeira Lopes, who was born in Vila Nova de Gaia then went on to become the director of Lisbon's Contemporary Art Museum. The collection contains a selection of Macedo's sculptures in a variety of styles as well as some of his personal collection of contemporary paintings and sculptures, including works by Carlos Botelho and Amadeo Sousa Cardoso. The tour ends in Teixeira's studio, with beautiful blue-tiled walls, amid his sculptures cast in bronze and marble and several giant plaster models. Guided tours of the museum are mandatory: you don't have to book, but it's a good idea to phone ahead to check if an English-speaking guide is available.

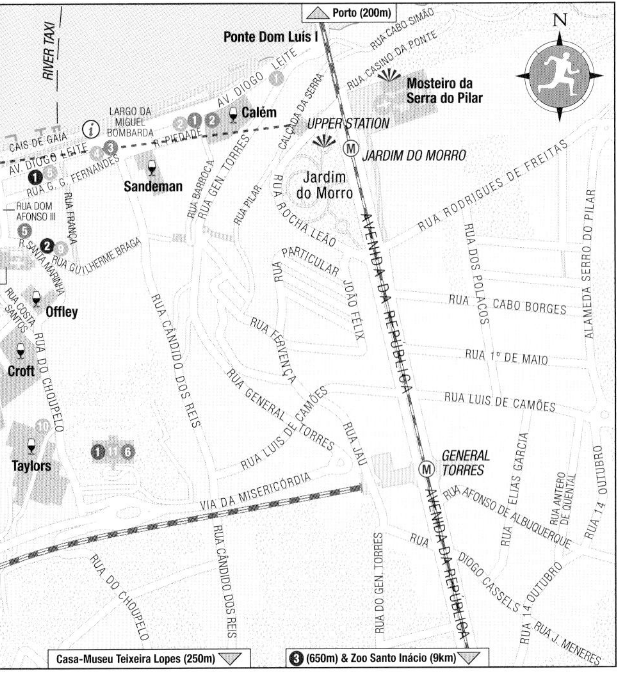

The port wine story

For three centuries, wine from Portugal's Douro region has been shipped down the river to Vila Nova de Gaia, whose famous wine lodges (Sandeman, Graham's, Cockburn and Taylor's) reflect the early British influence on its production. A **cellar tour** here (see below) forms an integral part of any Porto visit, and you can also follow the wine trail inland along the Douro by train, car or cruise boat (see box, p.67). To find out more, the country's port wine institute, the Instituto dos Vinhos do Douro e do Porto (Ⓦ ivdp.pt), has a useful English-language website, while the Rota do Vinho do Porto details the region's wine estates, attractions and events.

The clear distinction between **port wine** (vinho do porto) and other Portuguese wines wasn't made until the beginning of the eighteenth century, when Britain prohibited the import of French wines during the War of the Spanish Succession. Portuguese wines quickly filled the void and, following the **Methuen Treaty** (1703), the wine trade became so profitable that adulterated inferior wines were soon being passed off as the genuine article. This led to the creation of a regulatory body in 1756, the **Companhia Geral da Agricultura das Vinhas do Alto Douro**, and, the following year, the declaration of the world's oldest **demarcated wine region** (where port wine could now only legitimately be produced). Yet it wasn't until the mid-nineteenth century that it began to resemble today's fortified wine, when the addition of brandy to stop fermentation became widespread, enabling the wines to be transported over even longer distances.

The port wine lodges

Vila Nova de Gaia's *raison d'être*, of course, is the **port wine trade** – you can't miss the dozens of historic company lodges and warehouses (known as *caves*) that splash their brand names across every rooftop, facade and advertising hoarding. They almost all offer **tastings and tours**, conducted in a variety of languages including English, with a view to enticing you to buy. Tours of the smaller, lesser-known companies tend to be more personal than those of larger producers, but they are all pretty informative and you'll soon know the difference between a tawny and a ruby, and which vintages are best.

Around thirty **port wine lodges** in Vila Nova de Gaia are open for tastings. Many of the lodges are no longer independent but are owned by a parent company: Kopke, Burmester, Cálem and Barros for example belong to the Sogevinus brand, while Graham's, Cockburn's, Dow and Warre all belong to the Symington family, and Sogrape is the parent company of Offley, Ferreira and Sandeman. Most of the lodges are open daily all year round, though some close in the winter: almost all charge a fee for their tours with the price depending on the ports chosen for the tastings – usually €10 will get you a tour plus tasting of two ports, though if you want to taste more ports, and some of the pricier vintages, you'll pay extra. Most lodges run a system whereby you can just turn up for a tour, though this will be run in the language of the first person to book onto the tour. If you find that the next tour isn't in English, you may have to wait or book (in person or via the websites) onto a later tour.

If you don't have time for a full tour, there are several places that are not actual lodges, but do **port tastings**, including Sogevinus (see p.71), Kopke House (see p.70) and Quevedo Cellar (see p.71). Some of these do chocolate and olive oil tastings too, so you can skip all the historical stuff and just head straight for the sofas for some sipping and sampling.

Cálem

MAP p.62, POCKET MAP E9–F9
Av Diogo Leite 344 ⓣ 223 746 660, ⓦ calem.pt. Daily: April–Oct 10am–6.30pm; Nov–March 10am–6pm. Tours €10.

The nearest port wine lodge to the bridge, and therefore one of the most visited, **Cálem** nevertheless has a good visitor centre, and is especially informative about the port-wine's history and production process – you even watch a video about port from inside a vast converted oak vat. Tours last about 45 minutes and start in the lodge museum, then proceed through the cellars, ending up with the tasting. Pre-book if you want to make sure you get an English-language tour. They also hold fado concerts in the cellars (see p.71).

Churchill's

MAP p.62, POCKET MAP A8–B8
Rua do Fonte Nova 5 ⓣ 223 744 193, ⓦ churchills-port.com. Mon–Sat 10am–6pm. Tours €3.

One of the smallest lodges offering the least expensive and shortest of the cellar tours (20min), but a good choice if you want a basic background to the production process and the chance to sample three different ports.

Croft

MAP p.62
Rua Barão de Forrester ⓣ 412, 220 109 825, ⓦ croftport.com. Daily 10am–6pm. Tours €10.

Founded in 1588, Croft is the oldest company still making port today. Lined with giant barrels, the stone-clad reception room is where you begin the short thirty-minute tours led by very well-informed guides who take you round the old cellars. You can try three ports either in an atmospheric tasting room or on the small terrace in summer, which has fine views across the other lodges.

Cálem

Ferreira

MAP p.62, POCKET MAP B9
Av Ramos Pinto 70 ☎ 223 746 106. Daily 10am–12.30pm & 2–6pm. Tours €10.

The only major port house to have remained wholly under Portuguese control, Ferreira was founded in 1751, and is unusual in that it was a woman who was responsible for much of the company's success. Antónia Adelaide Ferreira, known as Ferreirinha, ran the company from the age of 33 (when her first husband died) until her death in 1896. After a thirty- to forty-minute tour of the cellars where you can marvel at the giant vats, tastings (two ports) take place in a cavernous vaulted room.

Graham's

MAP p.62, POCKET MAP A9
Rua do Agro 141 ☎ 223 776 484, Ⓦ grahams-port.com. Daily 9.30am–6pm; last tour 5.30pm. Tours €12.

It's a steep walk up to Graham's, which was originally founded by a Scottish family, and now owned by the Anglo/Scottish/Portuguese Symington wine dynasty. The thirty- to forty-minute tour includes a video and slide show plus a visit to a light and airy museum with interesting artefacts on display such as one of Winston Churchill's invoices showing his fondness for port and an 1887 Phillippe Patak watch made for the Queen of Portugal. The still-working cavernous cellars below house some two thousand barrels of ageing port, plus numerous bottles of the vintage stuff. The tour ends in the splendid tasting room with great views and a terrace overlooking the river. The lodge is also home to the highly rated *Vinum* restaurant (see p.70).

Graham's

Offley

MAP p.62
Rua do Choupelo 54 ☎ 223 743 852, Ⓦ eng.sograpevinhos.com. March–Oct daily 10am–12.30pm & 2–6pm. Tours from €6.

Although the company was founded in 1737 by William Offley, the man who most influenced it was Joseph James Forrester, later Baron de Forrester, an English wine merchant who ran the company from the 1830s. Although it's not open year-round, this is one of the cheapest lodges to visit: cellar tours with a tasting of two ports cost €6, though if you want to try more ports you can take the Reserve (€7.50 for three ports) or Baron of Forrester tours (€16 for various ports).

Ramos Pinto

MAP p.62, POCKET MAP D9
Av Ramos Pinto 380 ☎ 223 707 000, Ⓦ ramospinto.pt. Daily 10am–6pm. Tours €6.

In an attractive riverside building dating from 1880, this distinctive port lodge has a good museum housed in its 1930s' period offices – here you can learn about the history of this Portuguese company whose famous advertising posters did much to

The Douro wine route

Portugal's port wine grapes are grown in a 600,000-acre demarcated region along both banks of the Rio Douro, stretching from Mesão Frio (near Peso da Régua) to the Spanish border. Sheltered by the Marão and Montemuro mountain ranges, around fifteen percent of the region is under vines, which benefit from cold winters and hot, dry summers. The characteristic terraces can be seen along the length of the Douro, and they form a beautiful backdrop to the small town of Pinhão, which is now the main centre for quality ports. The grapes are harvested at the *quintas* (vineyard estates) from September to October and are then crushed. After a few days, fermentation is halted by the addition of brandy – exactly when this is done determines the wine's sweetness – with the wine subsequently stored in casks until the following March. The final stage in the wine process is its transportation downstream to the shippers' lodges, where the wine is blended and matures. One of the most scenic ways to visit the wine route is by train, along the Linha do Douro (see box, p.41), while drivers can follow the useful map at dourowinetourism.com, which details wine lodges to visit and *quintas* to stay at. River cruises along the Douro are detailed in Essentials (see box, p.127).

popularize port in the 1900s. One of the cheapest lodges, its tours include a trip to the extensive cellars where the port is aged and end, of course, with a tasting session of two ports: they leave every forty minutes or so, last around forty minutes, and can be booked at the visitor centre.

Sandeman

MAP p.62, POCKET MAP E9
Sandeman Terrace, Largo Miguel Bombarda sandeman.eu. Daily: March–Oct 10am–12.30pm & 2–6pm; Nov–Feb 9.30am–12.30pm & 2–5.30pm. Tours from €10.

The black-hat-and-cape cut-out provides the most recognizable of company logos and this ancient company certainly makes the most of its figure, with its tour guides dressed up as the distinctive Sandeman Don. In summer, drinks and food are served on a pleasant riverfront terrace in the front of the lodge. Tour prices start at €10 for a thirty-minute tour including a tasting of two ports, or you can opt for the 1790 tour (45min–1hr; €20) and sample five ports of a higher quality. It's best to book to ensure an English-language tour.

Taylors

MAP p.62
Rua do Choupelo 250 223 742 800, taylor.pt. Daily: April–Nov 10am–7.30pm; Dec–March 10am–6.30pm. Last entry 1hr 30min before closing. Tours €12.

Founded in 1692, and still an independent family firm, Taylor's provides an entertaining self-guided audio-tour (roughly 1hr) of its three-hundred-year-old cellars which have been renovated to include some modern and informative museum exhibits. The tour ends with a tasting of two ports, either in the attractive tasting room or in the pretty gardens and terrace with its panoramic views over the city: if you want to linger further over the view, or sample more their of their offerings, you can stay for a meal at the *Barão de Fladgate* restaurant (see p.68).

Shops

3maisarte

MAP p.62
Largo Joaquim Magalhães 12 ⓣ 223 758 255. April–Sept daily 11am–7pm, Oct–March Mon–Sat 11am–7pm.

As well as being an appealing café (see below), this is also a gallery and shop selling work by local artists in an old warehouse, with a caravan operating as its office.

Casa do Galo

MAP p.62, POCKET MAP D9
Av Diogo Leite 50 ⓣ 910 657 172, ⓦ acasadogalo.com. April–Sept daily 10am–10pm, Oct–March daily 10am–7.30pm.

Arts and crafts shop selling locally designed ceramics and wood-carving as well as tasteful cork bags and jewellery. It also does port tastings starting from €6 for three ports up to €40 for the top vintages.

3maisarte

El Corte Inglés

MAP p.62
Av da República 1435 ⓣ 223 781 400, ⓦ elcorteingles.pt; ⓜ Estação João de Deus. Mon–Sat 10am–11pm, Sun 10am–8pm.

Vast modern Spanish department store with six floors above ground and five below, selling pretty much anything you can think of. There's also an excellent supermarket. The café on the sixth floor is a good-value place for lunch with excellent views over the city.

Café

3maisarte

MAP p.62
Largo Joaquim Magalhães 12 ⓣ 223 758 255. April–Sept daily 11am–7pm, Oct–March Mon–Sat 11am–7pm.

At the bottom of the hill from *The Yeatman* (see p.70) this delightful tiny café-bar is technically more a multi-purpose community organization that sells local arts and crafts (see above), rescues cats, hires out bikes (€2.50/hr) and also serves wine and tapas. It's a perfect spot for a small lunchtime snack or to indulge your creative side over a glass of wine: expect to pay about €7 for a selection of cheeses, cold meats and a glass of wine.

Restaurants

Barão de Fladgate

MAP p.62
Taylor's, Rua do Choupelo 250 ⓣ 223 772 951. Mon–Sat 12.30–3pm & 7.30–10.30pm, Sun 12.30–3pm.

It's a punishing uphill hike to get here (unless you take a taxi), but once you get here you're rewarded by the finest river and bridge views from the terrace of Taylor's port wine lodge restaurant – it's a lovely spot

Beira Rio

for an alfresco lunch (two courses and a glass of wine for around €22). A fleet of smart waiters is on hand, but it's not really formal and not outrageously expensive either (à la carte pasta dishes cost from €16, fish and meat around €18–24). Many dishes have a slug of port in the recipe, while others (like duck leg with citrus risotto) make a change from the prevailing traditional Portuguese cuisine.

Beira Rio

MAP p.62, POCKET MAP D9
Av Diogo Leite 64 ⓣ 223 756 959. Mon, Tues & Thurs–Sun noon–10pm.

This appealing local restaurant is tiny inside but has tables outside on the riverfront, and friendly staff. It serves up local dishes, many simply grilled on the barbecue, such as chicken and sardines (€10) or salmon (€14), as well as the ubiquitous hearty *francesinha*.

Casa Adão

MAP p.62, POCKET MAP C9
Av Ramos Pinto 252 ⓣ 223 750 492. Daily noon–3.30pm & 7–11pm.

Simple family-run riverfront restaurant with low prices for grilled meat and fish (€8–14), with dishes ranging from steak and pork to salmon and sea bass. They also serve bigger platters of mixed grilled fish and the like, for two or more people (€20–30). Locals pack the place out at lunch (so there might be a wait for a table), and with house wine at €5 a litre there's not much work done in nearby offices in the afternoon.

Casa Dias

MAP p.62, POCKET MAP C9
Av Ramos Pinto 242 ⓣ 223 750 467. Daily 8am–midnight.

Casa Dias is a lovely tiled restaurant which features models of Porto's bridges on its walls. The main reason to visit here though, is for substantial portions of good-value food. Dishes of pork, grilled chicken or steaks come with mountains of chips (for around €8–10), or you can choose the fresh fish of the day, which costs from around €10.

De Castro

MAP p.62, POCKET MAP E9
Gaia Espaco Porto Cruz, Largo Miguel Bombarda 23 ⓣ 910 553 559, ⓦ myportocruz.com. Tues–Sat 12.30–4pm & 7.30–11pm, Sun 12.30–4pm.

On the third floor of the modern Espaço Porto Cruz building, this restaurant serves sandwiches, salads and tapas (€6–10) at lunchtime, plus more substantial dishes in the evening, such as roast duck with mushrooms and port (main courses cost around €12–16) – all accompanied by lovely river views.

Dourum

MAP p.62, POCKET MAP F8
Av Diogo Leite 454 ⓣ 220 917 911. Daily noon–10pm.

This tiny, traditional restaurant has a few tables that spill on to the street outside and boasts great views of the river. Come here for the tasty tapas (€3–9), such as octopus salad and sautéed squid, or you can opt for a hearty main course, with dishes including grilled pork fillet or *bacalhau à bras* (both costing around €11).

Vinum

Taberninha do Manel

MAP p.62, POCKET MAP E9
Av Diogo Leite 308 ⓣ 223 953 549, ⓦ taberninhadomanel.com. Daily 10am–2pm.

Long-established traditional restaurant whose tables outside on the waterfront offer great views over to Porto. It serves reasonably priced *petiscos*, such as hot roast pork sandwiches (€6) and a tasty wild mushroom and bean stew (€8), as well as more substantial dishes and, of course, *francesinhas*.

Toca do Coelho

MAP p.62, POCKET MAP D9
Largo Sampaio Bruno 2 ⓣ 223 754 820. Mon–Sat 9am–8pm.

At the side of the market building, with seats on a cobbled side street, this tiny local restaurant rustles up good-value lunches. Pork, chicken and deliciously fresh *pescada* are around €6–7; there are good salads, too.

Vinum

MAP p.42
Graham's, Rua do Agro 141 ⓣ 220 930 417, ⓦ vinumatgrahams.com. Daily 12.30–4pm & 6.30–11pm.

This spacious restaurant sits at the front of the vast Graham's port lodge, with a terrace that offers far-reaching views over town. The service is sleek and the food is excellent: expect the likes of squid rice cooked in its own ink or suckling pig with truffles. Mains start at €25 and, of course, you'll be offered a Graham's port at the end of the meal. Reservations advised.

The Yeatman

MAP p.62
Rua do Choupelo ⓣ 220 133 100. Mon–Fri 7.30pm–11pm, Sat & Sun 1–3pm & 7.30–11pm.

With two Michelin Stars to its name, *The Yeatman*'s gourmet restaurant can lay claim to being the top dining room in Portugal. You'll be served by a fleet of waiters who are every bit as impressive as the views over town. You can choose four (€100) or six dishes (€130) from the menu, or opt for the full tasting "Gastronomic Experience" (€150). Dishes use largely local produce – sea urchins, turbot or swordfish with kumquats, for example, followed by sublime desserts such as chocolate tripe. Each dish is accompanied by one of the restaurant's eighty varieties of wine or port (around €50 extra).

Port tastings

Kopke House

MAP p.62, POCKET MAP E9
Av Diogo Leite 312 ⓣ 223 746 660, ⓦ kopkeport.com. Daily: May–Oct 10am–7pm; Nov–April 10am–6pm.

If sampling different types of port isn't decadent enough for you, the three-storey *Kopke House*, right on the riverside, specializes in port and chocolate pairing. Made in Porto by Arcádia (see p.54) since the 1930s, the chocolates have been specifically selected to complement the wines. They do organic olive oil tastings here too (€2). Tastings start at €2.20 for a port and chocolate pairing, up to €95 depending on the port.

Quevedo Cellar

MAP p.62, POCKET MAP 000
Rua de Santa Marinha 11
Ⓦ quevedoportwine.com. Daily 10am–7pm.

This small family-run port and wine producer has a relaxed tasting room, tucked away behind the main riverfront street, with a wood burner and a piano. Here you can sample individual glasses of port or wine from the family's vineyards along the Douro, or pay €5 for two ports.

Sogevinus

MAP p.62, POCKET MAP C9
Av Ramos Pinto 280 Ⓣ 223 746 660, Ⓦ sogevinus.com. Daily: May–Oct 10am–7pm; Nov–April 10am–6pm.

Right on the riverfront, the Sogevinus shop has a great selection of ports from its own brands including Burmester, Cálem, Kopke, Barros and Gilberts. Individual tastings start at €2, or from €10 for a selection of five ports, up to €64 for a choice of vintage ports.

Bars and nightlife

Caves Cálem

MAP p.62, POCKET MAP E9
Av Diogo Leite 344 Ⓣ 223 746 660, Ⓦ fadoinporto.com.
Tues–Sun: April–Oct at 6.30pm; Nov–March at 6pm. €18.50.

The Cálem port lodge puts on atmospheric fado concerts in its cellars, with Portuguese guitar and singers. Concerts also include a tour and port tasting.

Dick's Bar

MAP p.62
The Yeatman, Rua do Choupelo Ⓣ 220 133 100. Mon–Thurs & Sun 9am–1am, Fri & Sat 9am–2.30am.

Much less formal than *The Yeatman*'s restaurant (see opposite), *Dick's Bar* is a great place to treat yourself to a drink. You can choose from no fewer than 25,000 bottles of wine, not to mention a variety of port-based cocktails (from €11) – try the one with Grand Marnier, orange zest and mint leaves, and if you're feeling flush, opt for the 1863 Taylor's port at a mere €120 a glass. The smart decor features big comfy sofas and glass table-tops crammed with corks; there's also live music (Thurs–Sat 8.30pm–1am). However, the big draw here is the staggering city-view: settle down on the outside terrace, on a sofa, or by the fire pit, and watch the sun set over the city.

Terrace Lounge 360

MAP p.62, POCKET MAP E9
Espaço Porto Cruz, Largo Miguel Bombarda 23. Tues–Sat 12.30–9pm, Sun 12.30–6.30pm.

Head up to the top floor of the Espaço Porto Cruz complex to sample some port, or any other drink, at this open-air rooftop bar with great views – sunset is the best time to come as you can watch the lights slowly coming on over the river and city opposite.

Dick's Bar

Miragaia and Masserelos

West of the centre lie the appealing districts of Miragaia and Masserelos, many of whose streets tumble down steep slopes that line the River Douro. On Miragaia's earthy riverfront, the Museu dos Transportes e Comunicações, housed in the city's huge former customs' house, is the highlight of a cluster of engaging museums. Steeply uphill lies the extensive gardens of the Palácio de Cristal, a tranquil spot to while away an afternoon. Sharing the garden's stunning views over the Douro, the adjacent Museu Romântico da Quinta da Macierihna gives an insight into how Porto's wealthy port merchants once lived. Heading back into town, the Museu Nacional Soares dos Reis is one of Portugal's finest art museums.

Museu dos Transportes e Comunicações

MAP p.74, POCKET MAP B6
Rua Nova de Alfândega ⓣ 223 403 000, ⓦ www.amtc.pt. Tues–Fri 10am–1pm & 2–6pm, Sat, Sun & hols 3–7pm (last entry 1hr before closing. €7.50; Communications museum only €5; Engine of the Republic exhibition only €3; Cars in Space and Time exhibition only €3; ground floor of customs house free. Tram #1 from Infante, or bus #500 from São Bento.

The Neoclassical Alfândega, or customs house, was built on a former fishermen's beach between 1860 and 1880. It's a vast building that was originally designed to store the cargo of up to forty ships, but was imaginatively renovated in the late twentieth century by famous Porto architect Eduardo Souto de Moura and now houses the **Museu dos Transportes e Comunicações** (Transport and Communications Museum). You can look round the ground floor of the huge customs house with its grand public rooms and access to the riverbank behind for free, while the upper two floors house the museum and its various exhibitions. On the first floor, the imaginative **Communications museum** looks at how trade, TV and radio have helped communications with the rest of the world, with plenty of interactive displays that children will enjoy including a giant megaphone, some very bulky early computers, TVs and record players. In the western wing of the first floor, the **Engine of the Republic** exhibition displays some of the cars used by Portugal's presidents since the birth of the republic in 1910, from the early horse-drawn

Museu dos Transportes e Comunicações

carriages to the armoured Mercedes favoured by former dictator Salazar and the Rolls Royce Phantom III bought for England's Queen Elizabeth II's state visit in 1957. Look out for the distinctive POR numberplate that all the president's official cars carry. You can also view entertaining authentic news footage of the cars being used on state occasions. Although the captions are only in Portuguese for this exhibition, you can pick up an English-language guide at the desk.

The second floor houses the interesting **Car in Space and Time** exhibition which traces the development of the motor vehicle and includes the first ever car bought to Portugal in 1895 (a French Panhard). The exhibition is currently being rotated to include as many different vehicles from the museum's collection as possible, but you can expect to see such vehicles as an early Mini, a 1947 Rolls Royce, a Sinclair C5 and a replica of Michael Schumacher's Formula 3 racing car.

World of Discoveries

MAP p.74, POCKET MAP B6
Rua de Miragaia 106 ☎ 220 439 770, 🌐 worldofdiscoveries.com. Mon–Sat 10am–6pm, Sat, Sun & hols 10am–7pm, last entry 30min before closing; adults €14; 4–12 years €8; discounts for online tickets. Tram #1 from Infante, or bus #500 from São Bento.

Great for kids, this is an informative **museum** with interactive displays themed around the famous Portuguese explorers of the fifteenth and sixteenth centuries, such as Ferdinand Magellan, Vasco da Gama, Bartolomeu Dias and Henry the Navigator. Actors re-enact scenes of the swash-buckling explorers in replicas of the newly discovered lands. You can also explore a recreated shipyard to learn about

World of Discoveries

the vessels they travelled in and life on board the ships. The highlight of the museum, however, is an entertaining boat trip down an internal river, through tableaux of the exotic foreign lands discovered by the Portuguese, including Africa, India, Japan, Brazil and Macao.

Igreja de São Pedro de Miragaia

MAP p.74, POCKET MAP B6
Largo de São Pedro de Miragaia. Tues–Sat 3.30–7pm, Sun 10–11.30am. Free. Tram #1 from Infante, or bus #500 from São Bento.

Tucked away off Rua Miragaia, the beautiful blue-tiled Igreja de **São Pedro de Miragaia** was built in the 1830s on the site of a medieval church, one of the oldest in Porto. Inside, check out the ornate Rococo wooden and gilt carvings, as well as the impressive sixteenth-century Flemish Pentecost triptych.

Museu do Vinho do Porto

MAP p.74, POCKET MAP C11
Rua de Monchique 45–52 ⓣ 222 076 300. Mon–Sat 10am–5pm, Sun 10am–noon & 2–5pm. €2.20. Tram #1 from Infante, or bus #500 from São Bento.

Housed in an eighteenth-century former wine warehouse, the low-tech but interesting **Museu do Vinho do Porto** details the history of the port wine trade. In many ways, this is the history of Porto itself and the museum passionately tackles the subject – exhibits chart the development of the business, linking the trade with the fortunes of the major port-wine families and showing how, in just a matter of decades, the city grew to become synonymous with port-wine.

Museu do Carro Eléctrico

MAP p.74, POCKET MAP A10
Alameda Basílio Teles 51 ⓣ 226 158 185, ⓦ museudocarroelectrico.pt. Mon 2–6pm, Tues–Sun 10am–6pm. €8. Tram #1 from Infante, or bus #500 from São Bento.

Porto's trams #1 and #18 make a fitting halt on the riverside outside the **Museu do Carro Eléctrico** (Tram Museum). In the echoing spaces of a former power station, you can admire Iberia's oldest streetcar (1872) alongside lotsof other gleaming vintage specimens, many made by companies in Birkenhead or Preston in England which gave the trams the nickname "English Cars". Look out for the Vagoneta 80, used to carry fresh fish from the market in Matosinhos to Porto's central markets in the 1930s. Black and white photos also give an insight into the importance public transport had in the development of the city.

Ponte da Arrábida

MAP p.74
Porto Bridge Climb: Rua d'Ouro 680 ⓣ 968 837 351, ⓦ portobridgeclimb.com. Climbs lasting 45min take place daily

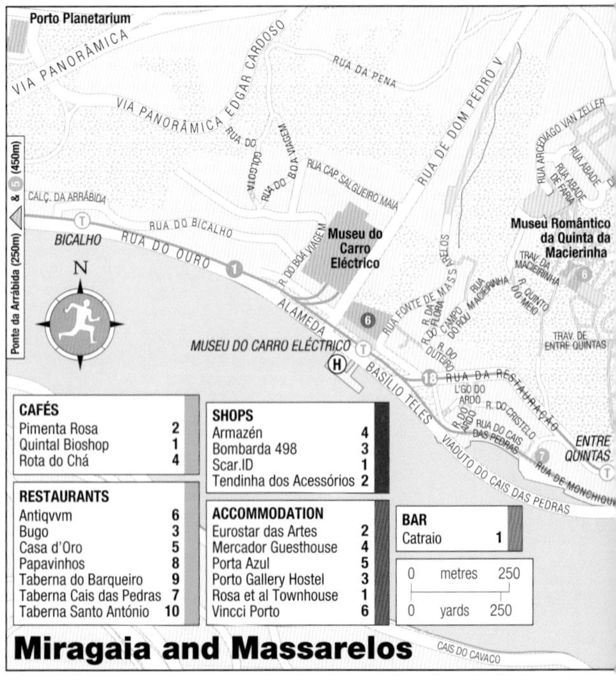

Porto's tram routes

Porto has three remaining **tram routes**, all of which are great fun to travel on. Tram #22 and #18 leave from the top of the Jardim da Cordoaria; #22 takes a circular route through the city centre via Torre dos Clérigos, Batalha and back via Aliados and the Igreja do Carmo, while #18 heads southwest to Masserelos, ending up by the Museu do Carro Eléctrico. If you only have time for one trip, choose tram #1. Starting from the end of Rua de Alfândega, it trundles alongside the river on a scenic twenty-five minute ride to Foz do Douro. Note that Andante passes are not valid on the trams (except for monthly passes); for details of tickets see Essentials (see p.123).

every 45min 2.30pm–dusk. Mon–Fri €9.50, Sat & Sun €12.50. Tram #1 from Infante, or bus #500 from São Bento.

Designed in 1963 by experimental engineer Edgar Cardoso, the arched **Pont da Arrábida** carries the busy A1 from Porto's Campo Alegre to the district of Arrábida. When it opened, it had the longest reinforced concrete bridge span in the world, at 270m. There's a small exhibition space at the foot of the bridge showing you how it was built. More exciting, however, is to climb the bridge with Porto Bridge Climb. The ascent involves a slow, steady and somewhat hairy climb up steps which take you to the top of the 70m-high central concrete arch. The view from the top is amazing, but make sure you wear sensible shoes and avoid wearing skirts or dresses, which can interfere with the harness.

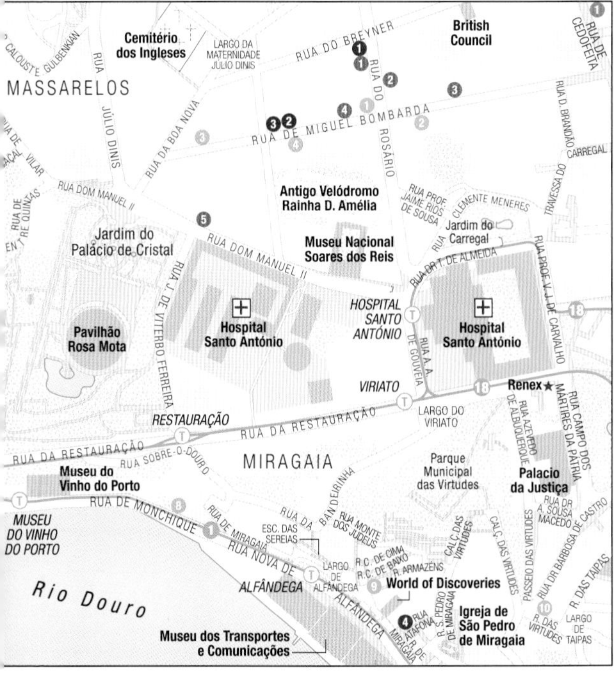

Jardim do Palácio de Cristal

MAP p.74, POCKET MAP A4
Rua Dom Manuel II ⓣ225 320 080. Daily: April–Sept 8am–9pm; Oct–March 8am–7pm. Free. Bus #200 from Aliados.

The attractive, landscaped **Jardim do Palácio de Cristal** is designed around the centrepiece Pavilhão Rosa Mota, which was named after Porto's best-known athlete and Olympic marathon runner. Resembling a kind of concrete tea cosy, the current pavillion was built in the 1950s to replace a far more elegant 1860s iron-and-glass "Crystal Palace". However the real draw here is the surrounding **gardens** that tumble down a steep hill and are dotted with areas of woodland. The gardens spread out over a series of terraces where peacocks parade around. There's an avenue of lime trees and stunning river views towards the Ponte da Arrábida and Foz beyond it from high vantage points on the south side. The municipal library is located near the main entrance, and a number of other buildings and galleries here put on exhibitions, workshops, summer concerts and children's activities. There's also a little kiosk café by the lake.

Museu Romântico da Quinta da Macieirinha

MAP p.74, POCKET MAP C10
Rua de Entre Quintas 220. Mon–Sat 10am–5.30pm, Sun 10am–12.30pm & 2–5pm. €2.50. Bus #200 from Aliados.

Originally built for a merchant's family in the nineteenth century, the **Quinta da Macieirinha** was bought by a port-wine millionaire, Antonio Ferreira Pinto Basto who used it as a summer house. He hosted a variety of illustrious guests here, including the King of Piedmont and Sardinia who stayed after his exile, and died here in 1849. The house has been renovated and refurnished with genuine furniture and artefacts from the period, giving a fascinating insight into life among Porto's wealthy nineteenth-century society. There's a billiard room, ballroom and private chapel and, as ever, the grounds are a beautiful, peaceful oasis with great views over the Douro.

Museu Nacional Soares dos Reis

MAP p.74, POCKET MAP B4
Rua Dom Manuel II 44 ⓣ 223 393 770, ⓦ museusoaresdosreis.pt. Tues–Sun 10am–6pm. €5, free on 1st Sun of the month.

A five-minute walk from the

Jardim do Palácio de Cristal

Jardim da Cordoaria, behind the hospital, stands the **Museu Nacional Soares dos Reis**. The oldest art museum in Portugal, it was founded in 1833 to preserve works confiscated from dissolved monasteries and convents. The present building, into which the collection was moved in the 1940s, was once a royal residence that served as the French headquarters in the Peninsular War.

The museum takes its name from sculptor **António Soares dos Reis** (1847–89), whose best-known work, *O Desterrado* (The Exile), is here, along with an extensive display of Portuguese art from the sixteenth to twentieth centuries. But it's the applied and decorative art that's perhaps most engaging – the museum contains excellent collections of gold jewellery, religious silverwork, Portuguese glassware, earthenware and textiles, delicate Chinese ceramics, noble French furniture and painted screens and laquered cabinets from the Far East. Special exhibitions concentrate on particular periods, artists or themes, and you could spend hours just browsing; there's also a (rather unkempt, but pretty) garden and a café, which serves a good-value daily lunch.

Rua Miguel Bombarda

The formerly run-down street of **Rua Miguel Bombarda** has transformed itself in recent years into the centre of Porto's arty, hipster and creative quarter. Home to contemporary art galleries, workshops, fashion boutiques, vintage shops, cafés and tea rooms, it's a good place to browse, though you won't find anything open much before mid-day, or on Sunday. Some of the street's more interesting galleries include the **Cruzes Canhoto**, at no. 452 (officially open daily 10am–7pm, but they rarely stick to this; phone ⓣ223 197 406 to check), where you can buy strange painted models and primitive, tribal and folk art; the upmarket **São Mamede** gallery at no. 624 (Tues–Fri 2–8pm, Sat 3–8pm), which sells sculptures by the likes of Victor Ribeiro for around €3500; and the more accessible **O Galeria**, at no. 61 (Mon–Sat noon–8pm), with changing exhibitions of paintings and sketches by artists such as Joanna Pinto, and a good range of more accessibly priced prints and illustrations for sale.

The street is also home to the **Centro Comercial Bombarda**, at no. 285 (Mon–Sat noon–8pm), where you can find a range of sometimes quirky independent shops selling everything from vintage clothing, toys, home-made jewellery and crafts to art, books, posters and vinyl. There are also food shops and a café (see p.78), plus a grassy courtyard to chill out in.

Inaugurações Simultâneas

Rua Miguel Bombarda and the streets around it are at their liveliest during the **Inaugurações Simultâneas** (literally, simultaneous openings), when many of the area's art galleries launch new shows, exhibitions and artists on the same day. The shops stay open in the evening and there's music, entertainment and performance art on the streets, which fill with art buffs, hipsters and the general public checking out the culture and events. They take place six times a year on a Saturday, starting at 4pm: check with the tourist board for the exact dates.

Armazén

Shops

Armazén

MAP p.74, POCKET MAP B6
Rua de Miragaia 93 ⓣ 222 011 702. Daily 11.30am–8pm.

An Aladdin's cave of antiques, bric-à-brac and retro furniture, this converted warehouse contains shops, stalls, workshops and galleries, selling everything from old-fashioned typewriters and antique picnic hampers to retro crockery and even a tuk-tuk. Sit round the fireplace at the café, or play baby-foot in the patio bar.

Bombarda 498

MAP p.74, POCKET MAP A3
Rua Miguel Bombarda 498 ⓣ 223 229 634. Mon–Fri 11.30am–7pm, Sat 3–7pm.

Designer boutique selling reasonably priced bags and clothes plus trendy brands such as Tanya Heath shoes, with their signature detachable heels that come in different styles and heights, and A Favela do Biquini, with its Brazilian (ie rather skimpy) swimwear.

Scar.ID

MAP p.74, POCKET MAP B3
Rua do Rosário 253 ⓣ 222 033 087, ⓦ scar-id.com. Mon–Sat 10am–8pm.

Trendy shop/gallery selling jewellery, ceramics, furniture and clothing by up-and-coming Portuguese designers. It's not cheap, but there are some really interesting and unusual pieces here – and you may pick up a bargain from the next big name.

Tendinha dos Acessórios

MAP p.74, POCKET MAP A3
Rua Miguel Bombarda 468 ⓣ 935 015 271. Tues–Sat 12.30–7.30pm.

Attractive shop selling women's clothes made by local designers at reasonable prices, as well as a few secondhand and vintage items. Also sells soaps by Viseu company, Só Sabão, made from local, natural ingredients. There's also a branch in Foz, at Rua de Gondarém 247.

Cafés

Pimenta Rosa

MAP p.74, POCKET MAP B3
Loja 14, CCBombarda, 285 Rua Miguel Bombarda ⓣ 933 662 289. Mon–Sat 10am–9pm.

Inside the CCBombarda shopping mall, this canteen-style restaurant serves excellent -alue buffet meals with salads, quiche, meat dishes, fish or pizza. Any dish of the day, with salad and a coffee costs just €4.70. The cakes are great too – particularly the chocolate – and come in huge portions.

Quintal Bioshop

MAP p.74, POCKET MAP B3
Rua do Rosario 177 ⓣ 222 010 008. Mon–Sat 10.30am–8pm.

Lovely little health-food-shop-meets-vegetarian-café selling a variety of organic and eco-friendly

Michelin-star cuisine and the importance of grandmas

In recent years, the Porto area has become a **culinary hotbed** with several Michelin Star chefs flying the flag for regional ingredients. Ricardo Costa's creative take on traditional cuisine has bought two Michelin Stars to *The Yeatman* (see p.70), using cooking skills passed down from his grandmother. With one Michelin Star, Vítor Matos also uses regional produce in the splendidly ornate *Antiqvvm* (see p.80). Out near the seafront, Pedro Lemos also claims to have taken inspiration from his grandmother who sold fish at the market in Matosinhos: unsurprisingly, the menu at his restaurant *Pedro Lemos* (see p.98) is excellent for fish and seafood dishes. Just north of Porto, at the wonderful seafront *Casa de Chá da Boa Nova* (see p.97), Porto-born Rui Paula reinterprets recipes used by – you guessed it – his grandmother, and has garnered a Michelin Star for it. Finally, at *Largo do Paço* (see p.110) out in Amarante, André Silva has retained the Michelin Star formerly obtained by his mentor V í tor Matos.

While all these restaurants are undoubtedly pricey, they are less expensive than UK equivalents – and all are worth splashing out on. If they are still beyond your budget, head to the Porto outpost of Lisbon-based, Michelin-Star chef, José Avillez: here, in the heart of Porto, the *Cantinho do Avillez* bistro (see p.57) serves up interesting and innovative contemporary Portuguese food at affordable prices.

food and products. The café at the back serves veggie and vegan food, including soups, tofu sandwiches, beanburgers and juices, and there's also a pretty garden.

Rota do Chá

MAP p.74, POCKET MAP A3
Rua Miguel Bombarda 457 ⓣ 220 136 726, ⓦ rotadocha.pt. Mon–Fri 11am–8pm, Sat 11am–9pm, Sun noon–8pm.

Tucked behind a shop that sells a variety of loose leaf teas, plus colourful tins and caddies of exotic brews, is a hideway tea room in a pretty Eastern garden, dotted with giant buddhas, low tables with shaded seats and arbours. It's a great place for a lazy afternoon with a book, a big pot of fancy leaves and a *tosta* (€3), or the dish of the day, such as prawn rice (€7).

Scar.ID

Restaurants

Antiqvvm

MAP p.74, POCKET MAP C10
Rua de Entre Quintas 220 ⓣ 226 000 445, ⓦ antiqvvm.pt.

Beautifully positioned in a corner of the Jardim do Palácio de Cristal, with its own little garden offering stunning Douro views, this is one of Porto's most alluring restaurants. Chef Vítor Matos (see box, p.79) has earned the nineteenth-century former *quinta* a Michelin Star. You can choose from the tasting menu or go à la carte (though both are at least €100). Expect the likes of scallop and champagne ravioli, mussels escabeche, or black pork with Douro red wine sauce, all with top Portuguese wines.

Bugo

MAP p.74, POCKET MAP A3
Rua Miguel Bombarda 598 ⓣ 226 062 179, ⓦ bugo.com.pt. Mon–Thurs noon–3pm & 7.30–11pm, Fri noon–3pm & 7.30pm–midnight, Sat 12.30–4pm & 7.30pm–midnight.

Seriously good burgers, made from free-range meat, sourced from Portuguese farmers. You can choose from chicken, beef, tuna, sausage or chickpea burgers, and can opt for a variety of gourmet-style toppings, including goat's cheese; pineapple and bacon; port, prosciutto and cheese; or sautéed turnip greens and chestnut sauce. The burgers start at €8 and come with chips – if you choose not to have the bun, you get extra rice or roasted potatoes as well as chips.

Casa D'Ouro

MAP p.74
Rua Ouro 797 ⓣ 226 106 012. Tues–Thurs 12.30–3pm & 8–11pm, Fri–Sun 12.30pm–midnight.

This excellent Italian restaurant and pizzeria couldn't get much closer to the river, with a superb outdoor terrace facing the Ponte de Arrábida – indeed, the engineers were housed in the building when they constructed it. Authentic Italian cuisine features the likes of *ossobuco alla Milanese* (veal with a vegetable and wine sauce) and a range of pasta and pizzas (from €8–14), not to mention desserts including a sumptuous tiramisu.

Papavinhos

MAP p.74, POCKET MAP A6 & D11
Rua de Monchique 23 ⓣ 222 000 204. Tues–Sun noon–3pm & 7–10.30pm.

Just up from the Museu dos Transportes e Comunicações

Rota do Chá

Antiqvvm

and on the route of tram #1, this contemporary restaurant is on two floors, with fine river views from the top one. The innovative menu features the likes of spicy clams, mussels and a long list of fresh fish and meat (from €10–14), together with a fine and filling *arroz de marisco* (around €28 for two).

Taberna do Barqueiro

MAP p.74, POCKET MAP B6
Rua de Miragaia 123–124 ⓣ 937 691 732.
Mon–Sat noon–3pm & 7–11pm.

A small, friendly local tavern with tables out on the pretty square opposite the Museu dos Transportes e Comunicações. It's an alluring spot for a glass or two of Douro red wine and a range of tapas (*pataniscas*, *alheira*, hams and local cheeses), all from around €4–6. It also serves tasty mains (grilled meat or fish of the day) from €9–13. The interior is cosy but small, so best to reserve.

Taberna do Cais das Pedras

MAP p.74, POCKET MAP C11
Rua de Monchique 65–68 ⓣ 913 164 584.
Tues–Sun noon–2am.

In a lovely tiled building with a solitary palm tree at the front, this local restaurant serves traditional Porto cuisine in very reasonably sized tapas-style portions – dishes you can choose from include octopus, clams, *chouriço* and snails. It has *azulejos* in the cosy interior and there's a terrace outside overlooking the river. Wine comes in ceramic jugs. Expect to pay around €18 a head.

Taberna Santo António

MAP p.74, POCKET MAP C6
Rua das Virtudes 32 ⓣ 222 055 306.
Tues–Sun noon–3.30pm & 7.30–10pm.

This is a tiny tavern from the Porto old school, with half a dozen paper-topped tables crammed into the dining room. The menu features just two daily meat and two daily fish dishes – expect the likes of simply grilled chicken or *bacalhau* – and at under €5 for a hearty main course, it's hard to fault.

Bar

Catraio

MAP p.74, POCKET MAP C3
Rua de Cedofeita 256 ⓣ 934 360 070.
Tues–Thurs 4pm–midnight, Fri & Sat 4pm–2am.

Part bar and part shop, *Catraio* specializes in craft beers from microbrewers around Portugal and beyond. If you thought Portuguese beer consisted of only Super Bock and Sagres, think again: here you can sample stouts, amber ales and many others, with the week's specials chalked up on a board. The Sovina chestnutty brown ale is a good one to start with.

Boavista and the west

The highlight of the well-to-do suburb of Boavista is the Casa da Música, Porto's main cultural centre and its most stunning chunk of modern architecture. Equally impressive are Iberia's largest synagogue, the Sinagoge Kadoorie, and the expansive magnolia-lined Cemitério de Agramonte. It's a short ride west to the leafy Jardim Botânico do Porto, while there are further architectural attractions in the form of the Fundação Serralves, where buildings house contemporary art exhibitions in extensive grounds. The area's other attractions include the lively Bom Sucesso market, one of Portugal's oldest churches, Igreja de São Martinho de Cedofeita, and Boavista FC, the city's second football club.

Jardim Botânico do Porto

MAP p.84

Rua do Campo Alegre 1191 ⓣ 220 408 727, ⓦ jardimbotanico.up.pt. Mon–Fri 9am–6pm, Sat, Sun & hols 10am–6pm. Free. Bus #200 from Aliados.

Part of the University of Porto, the attractive **botanical gardens** were laid out in 1951. The gardens are an appealing mixture of the formal and the wild, with steps and paths leading up through plants from different habitats. Topiary, rose gardens and the most formal gardens are centred around the elegant **Casa Andresen**, named after the owners of the estate before it was given to the state. Beyond here there's an arid zone, with various cacti and succulents as well as greenhouses with larger cacti and beautiful orchids. Then, further down the hill you'll find a lake and mature trees, including magnolias that are magnificent in early spring.

Sinagoge Kadourie

Sinagoge Kadoorie

MAP p.84

Rua de Guerra Junqueiro 340 ⓣ 911 768 596. Guided tours by appointment only €5. Ⓜ Casa da Música.

Despite Portugal being an overwhelmingly Catholic country, Porto is home to Iberia's largest synagogue, the **Sinagoge Kadourie** with its impressive Art Deco facade. It was founded largely due to the efforts of Captain Barros Basto, a World War I veteran, who was surprised to discover his heritage when his grandfather confessed to being Jewish on his deathbed in the 1920s. During the sixteenth-century inquisitions, Jews had been forced to convert to New Christians and open worship was difficult until the twentieth century. So Barros Basto began a campaign to reconvert New

Cemitério de Agramonte

Christians back to the Jewish faith, travelling round Portugal by donkey to do so; he also taught himself Hebrew and set up a Jewish newspaper, *Halapid*. With the support of prominent Jews around Europe (including Baron de Rothschild of Paris), he raised the funds to build "the cathedral of the north", as he called the Kadourie synagogue. Ironically, the Sinagoge Kadourie opened in 1938, the same year that other synagogues were being ransacked by Nazi Germany. You can find out more about the synagogue and Captain Barros Basto in the small museum here.

Cemitério de Agramonte

MAP p.84
Rua de Agramonte ⓣ 226 066 604. Daily 8.30am–5pm. Free. Ⓜ Casa da Música.
Built in 1855 in response to a cholera epidemic, the **Cemitério de Agramonte** was a simple burial ground until the 1870s when elaborate mausoleums began to be built. These became ever more extravagant with the cemetery becoming the resting-place of choice for Porto's wealthy, as well as for writers, artists and musicians, including painter António Carneiro, violinist Guillermina Suggia, photographer Emílio Biel and architect Tomás Soller.

It's a tranquil and interesting place to explore: stroll along the magnolia-lined paths, and admire the enormous, ornate mausoleums, some boasting sculptures by the likes of Soares dos Reis, António Teixeira Lopes and Alves Pinto. Also, peer into the impressive, if rather eerie, oval-shaped Jazigo Municipal (the municipal burial building), built in granite and iron, where the city's poorer citizens were buried stacked on shelves.

Mercado do Bom Sucesso

MAP p.84
Praça Bom Sucesso 3 ⓣ 226 056 610. Market Mon–Sat 9am–8pm; food stalls, restaurants and bars Mon–Thurs & Sun 10am–11pm, Fri & Sat 10am–midnight. Ⓜ Casa da Música.
Originally built in the 1950s as a fresh produce market, the renovated **Mercado do Bom Sucesso** now houses food stalls, boutique shops, cafés and bars, plus a small section selling fruit and veg – there's even a hotel (see p.117). The impressive, hangar-like structure is big enough to park a plane or two. It's a great place for lunch, with everything from pizza and vegetarian food (see p.88) to seafood and sushi – the stall with the longest lunchtime queue is *Leitão do Zé*, which sells rolls filled with spit-roast suckling pig and chips for a bargain €5. There's entertainment in the evenings, with live music, DJs and workshops.

Boavista and the west

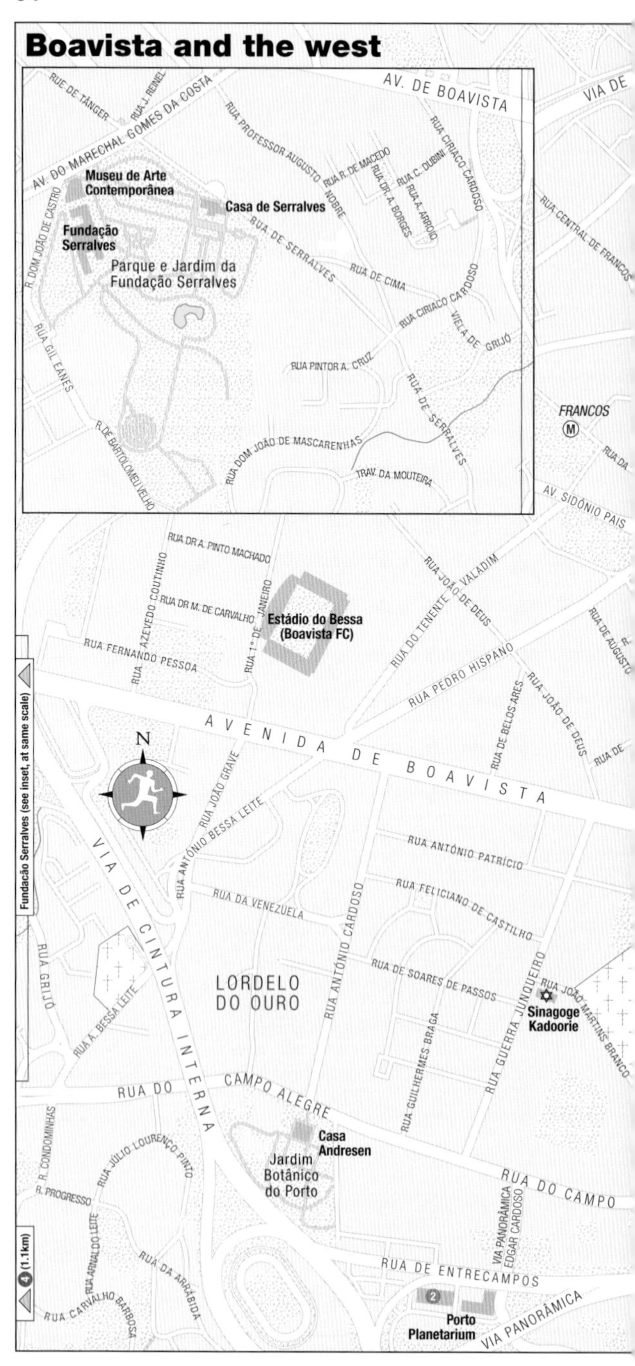

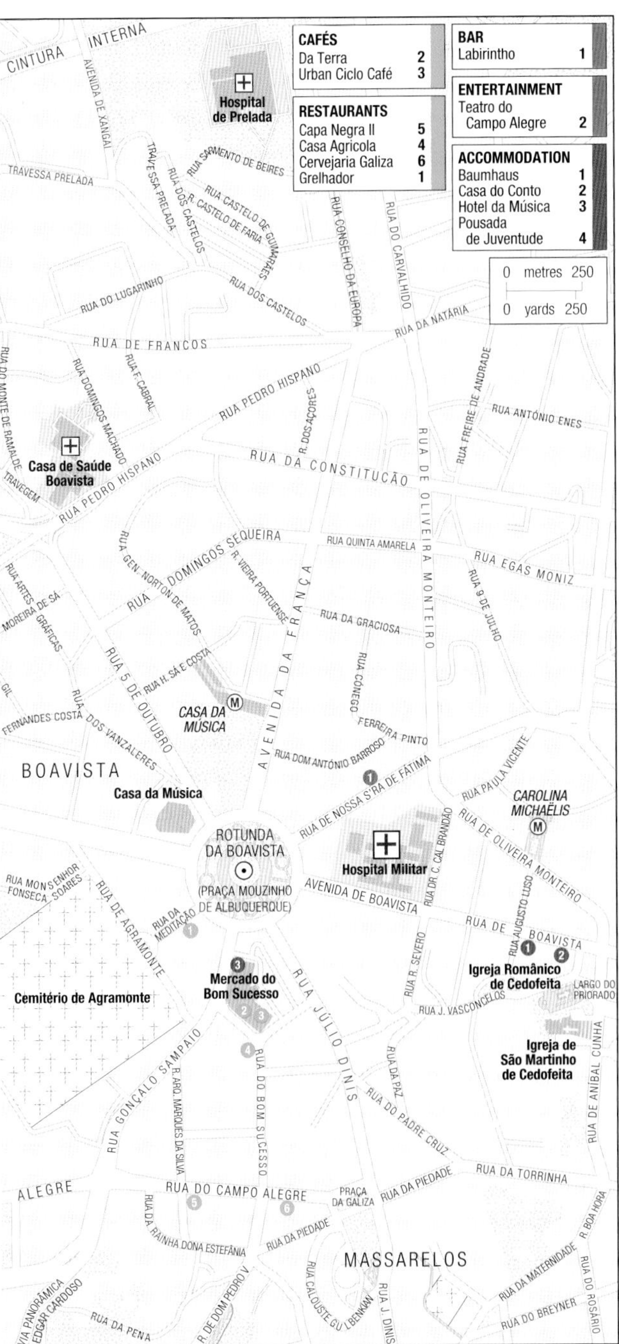
CAFÉS
Da Terra 2
Urban Ciclo Café 3
RESTAURANTS
Capa Negra II 5
Casa Agricola 4
Cervejaria Galiza 6
Grelhador 1
BAR
Labirintho 1
ENTERTAINMENT
Teatro do Campo Alegre 2
ACCOMMODATION
Baumhaus 1
Casa do Conto 2
Hotel da Música 3
Pousada de Juventude 4
0 metres 250
0 yards 250
CINTURA INTERNA
Hospital de Prelada
Casa de Saúde Boavista
BOAVISTA
Casa da Música
CASA DA MÚSICA
ROTUNDA DA BOAVISTA
(PRAÇA MOUZINHO DE ALBUQUERQUE)
Hospital Militar
CAROLINA MICHAËLIS
Cemitério de Agramonte
Mercado do Bom Sucesso
Igreja Românico de Cedofeita
Igreja de São Martinho de Cedofeita
LARGO DO PRIORADO
MASSARELOS
PRAÇA DA GALIZA
AVENIDA DA FRANÇA
AVENIDA DE BOAVISTA
RUA DE FRANCOS
RUA PEDRO HISPANO
RUA DA CONSTITUCÃO
RUA DE OLIVEIRA MONTEIRO
RUA DOMINGOS SEQUEIRA
RUA EGAS MONIZ
RUA DE BOAVISTA
RUA JÚLIO DINIS
RUA DO CAMPO ALEGRE
RUA DO BOM SUCESSO
RUA DE AGRAMONTE
RUA GONÇALO SAMPAIO
RUA 5 DE OUTUBRO
RUA DA TORRINHA
RUA DA PIEDADE
RUA DO CARVALHIDO
RUA CONSELHO DA EUROPA
RUA DE ANÍBAL CUNHA
RUA DA NATÁRIA
RUA ANTÓNIO ENES
RUA DOS CASTELOS
RUA DO LUGARINHO
TRAVESSA PRELADA
RUA DE NOSSA S'RA DE FÁTIMA
RUA DO PADRE CRUZ
RUA DA RAINHA DONA ESTEFÂNIA
RUA DA PENA
RUA DO BREYNER
RUA DA MATERNIDADE
RUA DO ROSÁRIO

The other Porto football team

Less well known than their city rivals Porto, **Boavista** actually have an impressive pedigree. Founded in 1903, the club has won five Portuguese Cups and one Championship, in 2001, making them only the second Portuguese team to ever win it outside the top teams of Porto, Sporting or Benfica. The 2004 construction of the impressive Estádio do Bessa , for the European Championships, proved to be the start of a rocky time for the club. Steeped in debt, Boavista were then found guilty of bribery and were relegated to the second tier in 2008. It was not until 2014 that the club had sufficient funds to be allowed back into the top division.

Rotunda da Boavista

The northwestern edge of the city centre – 2km from downtown Aliados – is marked by the large park-cum-roundabout, which is called the Praça Mouzinho de Albuquerque, but is more commonly known as the **Rotunda da Boavista**. The mighty obelisk in the centre commemorates the defeat of the French in the Peninsular War (1808–14), with a Portuguese lion squatting on top of a vanquished French eagle. Despite the swirling traffic, the rotunda is a pleasant place to rest from the heat under the trees. It also marks the start of Porto's longest road, the 5km-long Avenida da Boavista, which runs all the way out to the coast at Foz do Douro.

Igreja de São Martinho de Cedofeita

MAP p.84, POCKET MAP B1
Largo do Priorado, off Rua Aníbal Cunha ⓣ 222 000 635. Tues–Fri 4–7pm. Free. Ⓜ Lapa or Ⓜ Carolina Michaelis.

Located a few blocks off the Rotunda is the very simple **Igreja de São Martinho de Cedofeita**, which some claim has its origins as far back as the ninth century AD – making it one of the oldest churches in Iberia. However, the existing Romanesque building is a thirteenth-century remodelling of a church whose existence can only be dated with certainty to 1087. Whatever its origins, Cedofeita is unique in being Portugal's only Romanesque church to have kept its original dome, which is supported by bulky exterior buttresses.

Casa da Música

MAP p.84
Av da Boavista 604–610 ⓣ 220 120 210, ⓦ casadamusica.com. One-hour guided tours daily at 11am and 4pm in English and Portuguese. Tours €7.50. Building and shop Mon–Sat 9.30am–7pm, Sun & hols 9.30am–6pm. Restaurant Mon–Thurs 12.30–3pm & 7.30–11pm, Fri & Sat 12.30–3pm & 7.30pm–midnight. Ticket office Mon–Sat 9.30am–7pm; most tickets cost €5–20, though some events are free. Ⓜ Casa da Música.

Rem Koolhaas' superb modern cultural centre, the **Casa da Música** – a vast white wedge on a bare esplanade – looks as if the Mother Ship has landed, an impression reinforced by the steel staircase leading up into the black mouth of the entrance. It's a striking building with undulating ground outside where BMX riders cycle, and walls that jut out at angles above your head. Porto's major concert hall, it opened to great fanfare in 2005 and now has an international reputation, not just for recitals and classical concerts – it's home of the Orquestra Nacional do Porto, one of the country's leading symphony orchestras – but for early and contemporary music, fado, world, jazz, folk and experimental music too. Attending a concert or event is clearly the best way to see the building, especially inside the 1300-seat Grand Auditorium with its glass walls, but there are daily, hour-long guided visits if you want to know more about its dramatic design and construction. There's also an impressive black-and-white tiled roof terrace and top-floor restaurant.

Estádio do Bessa

MAP p.84
Rua 1 de Janeiro, off Av da Boavista ⓣ 226 071 024, ⓦ boavistafc.pt. Bus #201 from Av dos Aliados, or Ⓜ Francos, which is 1km northeast of the stadium.

The modern, if compact, **Estádio do Bessa Século XXI** is home to Boavista, Porto's second football team. The 28,200-seat stadium was built for the 2004 European Championship, but the club rarely gets anything like that number of spectators so it is usually easy to get tickets for matches, even against the big boys such as Sporting or Benfica. It's a homely ground, and if you want to find out more about the club or the other sports that it runs (including boxing, volleyball and handball), there is a small museum at the stadium but this is only open on request.
Tickets (from around €20) can be bought on the day at the stadium or online on ⓦ boavistafc.pt.

Fundação Serralves

MAP p.84
Rua Dom João de Castro 210 ⓣ 226 156 500, ⓦ serralves.pt. April–Sept Mon & Wed–Fri 10am–7pm, Sat, Sun & hols 10am–8pm; Oct–March Mon & Wed–Fri 10am–6pm, Sat, Sun & hols 10am–7pm. Museum & park €10; additional fees for some exhibitions; park only €5; both free first Sun of the month 10am–1pm. Ⓜ Casa da Música, or bus #502 from Bolhão or bus #203 from Rotunda da Boavista.

If there's one must-see cultural attraction in Porto it's the contemporary art museum and park run by the Fundação Serralves, 4km west of the centre. The **Museu de Arte Contemporânea** is the work of Porto architect Álvaro Siza Vieira, and is a minimalist triumph of white facades and terraces strikingly set in an overwhelmingly green park. The museum holds 4300 artworks from the 1960s to the present day, though there is no permanent collection: instead several changing exhibitions a year draw on the works of Portuguese and international artists, such as Joan Miró. Other exhibitions are held in the separate, pink Art Deco **Casa de Serralves** in the grounds.

Fundação Serralves

You can get an idea of the main building from the outside, and from the terrace café, the more formal restaurant and the museum shop (all free to enter). And if the exhibitions aren't to your taste, you miss nothing by just visiting the expansive, surrounding **park**. Indeed, many people prefer this to the museum itself, and it's easy to spend a lazy afternoon here, winding along swept gravel paths and clipped lawns before descending wooded tracks to the herb gardens and farmland beyond, grazed by goats and cattle. There are art installations dotted around and a teahouse in a glade with a vine colonnade. July and August see a sequence of "Jazz no Parque" (Jazz in the Park) **concerts** held in the gardens.

Capa Negra II

Cafés

Da Terra

MAP p.84
Mercado do Bom Sucesso, Praça Bom Sucesso 3. Mon–Thurs & Sun 10am–11pm, Fri & Sat 10am–midnight.

Vegetarians should seek out the tiny *Da Terra*, which is tucked away in the far corner of the Bom Sucesso market – for €8.50 you can choose any (or all) of the daily selection of salads and tasty hot dishes, such as ratatouille, bean burgers, soya fillet in asparagus sauce, plus a soup and small drink. They also do lovely cakes and fresh juices, such as strawberry, banana and mint.

Urban Ciclo Café

MAP p.84
Rua do Bom Successo 18 ⓣ 912 362 356. Mon–Sat 10am–8pm.

Despite the city's hills, cycling is popular in Porto and the bike-café trend is catching on too. This cosy, stylish café, with bikes hanging from the ceiling, serves coffees, *tostas*, cakes and a good brunch as well as selling bikes and accessories and renting out bikes, electric bikes and doing repairs.

Restaurants

Capa Negra II

MAP p.84
Rua do Campo Alegre 191 ⓣ 226 078 383, ⓦ capanegra.com. Mon–Sat noon–2am, Sun noon–midnight.

A metal brewing still marks the entrance to this modern and extremely popular *cervejaria* – there are often queues to get in at weekends – which serves food until late. They champion their *francesinhas* but the steaks are just as good, or there's an extensive menu from shellfish and grilled chicken to omelettes; most mains are €10–€20 and portions are huge. Jump in a cab from the centre; it won't cost much to get here.

Casa Agricola

MAP p.84
Rua Bom Sucesso 241 ⓣ 226 053 350, ⓦ casa-agricola.com. Daily 10am–2am; restaurant Mon–Sat 10am–2am, bar daily 10am–2am.

Cosy café-restaurant in an eighteenth-century former merchant's house. The restaurant is all dark wood and chandeliers, with a broad menu featuring the likes of roast beef, monkfish rice with prawns and grilled octopus, black pork and duck risotto (mains around €16). The pub-like bar area is less formal and also has a few tables at the back, and features live jazz and blues after 10pm on Thursday till Saturday evenings.

Cervejaria Galiza

MAP p.84
Rua do Campo Alegre 55 ⓣ 226 084 442, ⓦ cervejariagaliza.pt. Daily 12.30pm–1.45am.

This popular, modern *cervejaria* serves up a delicious range of meat and seafood until 1am. The menu features pork chops, hake fillets and other grills from €8–14, and it also does a very filling *arroz de marisco* (€19). It's always bustling, with a TV in the corner usually showing the evening's football.

Grelhador

MAP p.84
Rua da Meditação 39 ⓣ 226 091 440. Daily 11am–midnight.

Near the Casa da Música, this is a pleasant, modern space for good-value Portuguese dishes: *alheira* and chicken are just €6, or opt for the excellent squid kebabs or mixed meat grills (chicken, pork and veal) from around €11, all chargrilled on a barbecue.

Bar

Labirintho

MAP p.84
Rua Nossa Senhora de Fátima 334 ⓣ 919 701 490, ⓜ Casa da Música. Daily 10pm–4am.

Just a couple of minutes off the Rotunda da Boavista, this cultural space has a great bar set in different quirky rooms in a converted house, with a shaded back garden. It also functions as gallery space and bookshop, with occasional live music, and usually attracts an arty young crowd.

Entertainment

Teatro do Campo Alegre

MAP p.84
Rua das Estrelas ⓣ 226 063 000, ⓦ teatromunicipaldoporto.pt. Daily 2.30–7pm & 7.30–10.30pm. Bus #200 from Aliados.

An innovative playhouse putting on a vibrant blend of music, theatre, cinema, animation and public lectures.

Da Terra

Foz do Douro, Matosinhos and Leça da Palmeira

Where the River Douro meets the Atlantic Ocean, Foz do Douro makes an excellent day-trip from Porto – or you could even base yourself here and explore the city by tram. Formerly a fishing port, it's now an affluent suburb with some pleasant sandy beaches, where locals enjoy cold swims in summer and blowy walks between its two sea forts in winter. It's also home to Porto's largest green space, the Parque de Cidade, and the enjoyable Sea Life aquarium. Neighbouring Matosinhos, its large beach aside, has a far more industrial skyline than Foz do Douro. Despite its unappealing appearance, the city has undergone something of a renaissance in recent years, with its own metro line connecting it to Porto and a swanky cruise terminal. The main draw here, though, is to visit one of its famed fish restaurants. Further north up the coast, the industrial town of Leça da Palmeira has a broad town beach for surfers, Portugal's second tallest lighthouse and the Piscina das Mares, natural rock pools that are ideal for swimming when the Atlantic gets too rough.

Foz Velha

Formerly the fishermen's quarter, the most historic part of Foz do Douro is called **Foz Velha** (old Foz), and sits southeast of the seafront facing the Douro estuary; tram #1 runs here from the city centre, stopping along the riverfront at its southern edges. Today, Foz is distinctly upmarket, even sheltering a Michelin-starred restaurant, *Pedro Lemos* (see p.98), and its back streets make a good place for a stroll past the pretty early eighteenth-century Igreja de Sao João de Douro and the affluent villas with their iron balconies and large gardens with lemon trees.

Jardim do Passeio Alegre

MAP p.92, POCKET MAP B13

Some of the nicest houses in Foz face onto the riverfront **Jardim do Passeio Alegre**, a pretty wedge-

Getting to Foz

The most fun route to Foz is to take **tram #1** from Ribeira, which trundles up the riverfront to Foz Velha, a ten-minute walk from the sea. Alternatively, you can take **bus** #500 from São Bento; bus #502 from Bolhão to Parque de Cidade; bus #203 from Rotunda da Boavista via Serralves museum, to central Foz and Castelo do Queijo; or #200 from Bolhão to Castelo do Queijo.

Foz do Douro seafront

shaped park, which was laid out in the early twentieth century. Fringed by towering palms, where troops of parakeets swoop and chatter, it has a couple of mini lakes, a children's play area, a mini golf course and a Sunday market, with stalls selling local produce and artesan products (10am–6pm). The park is also home to most ornate toilets in Portugal, set in a beautifully tiled Art Nouveau pavilion; built in 1910, they are still in use today – check out the Ladies, with their Art Deco peacock tiles and an original restored toilet and sink dating from 1888 and painted in blue (you can't use this, as it's just for show).

Igreja de São João Baptista

MAP p.92, POCKET MAP C13
Largo da Igreja ☎ 226 180 015. Tues–Sun 9am–noon & 3–7pm. Free.

The small, pretty white seventeenth-century **church of São João Baptista** is known for its ornate altarpieces and impressive Baroque side altars, beautifully decorated with intricately designed gilt-wood carvings.

Farol de São Miguel-o-Anjo

MAP p.92, POCKET MAP C13

Just southeast of the Jardim do Passeio Alegre, on a small promontory jutting into the river estuary, it is easy to overlook the squat, coarse-stone **Farol de São Miguel-o-Anjo**. However, this lighthouse is one of the oldest in Europe, dating back to 1528, when fires were lit at its summit to alert any approaching ships.

Castelo de São João Baptista

MAP p.92, POCKET MAP B13
Esplanada do Castelo ☎ 226 153 440.

Just beyond the Jardim do Passeio Alegre, the confluence of river and ocean is dominated by the **Castelo de São João**, a sixteenth-century sea fort, which was one of the first to be built in a star shape. The sea fort was modified the following century, but lost its strategic importance as the river shifted (it was originally situated right on the shoreline). Today the Castelo de São João belongs to the National Defence Institute and is only open for occasional exhibitions: check with the tourist office (see p.126) for details of what's on. You can take a stroll around the mouth of the estuary here, along the sea walls that run behind the fort, a favourite spot for the local fishermen.

Foz seafront

Though it can't claim to have Portugal's best beaches, Foz's **seafront** still attracts plenty of visitors: take care, however, as the sand is interspersed with rocks, and the Atlantic can get pretty wild and is cold. At the seafront's southern end, you can walk up to the **Farol de Felgueiras** lighthouse.

Heading north, Avenida do Brasil and Avenida do Montevideu are packed with bars, restaurants and cafes. A boardwalk and promenade stretch all the way to the Castelo do Queijo, just over 2km to the north, passing a series of coves: Praia do Molhe is the nicest. Along the promenade, you can stroll beneath the **Pergola da Foz**, built in the 1930s for the Mayor of Porto's wife, who had been so enchanted by the pergola on the Promenade des Anglais in Nice that she insisted that Porto should have its own. Here too is the **Homem do Leme statue**, dedicated to sea captains who navigate these tricky waters.

Mercado da Foz

MAP p.92, POCKET MAP B12
Rua de Diu. Mon–Fri 7am–7pm, Sat 7am–5pm.

With its interesting local food stalls, the revamped **Mercado da Foz** is a good place to head for an inexpensive lunch. In common with many others in Portugal, this small local market was struggling to survive, so has diversified: as well as the usual vegetable, fish, meat and flower stalls, it has several small independent cafés and restaurants specializing in local produce and different dishes, from salads, wraps and juices, to sweets (see p.96), a hamburger bar and the Famous Dog hot-dog stall.

Castelo do Queijo

MAP p.92
Praça do Gonçalves Zarco 226 181 067.

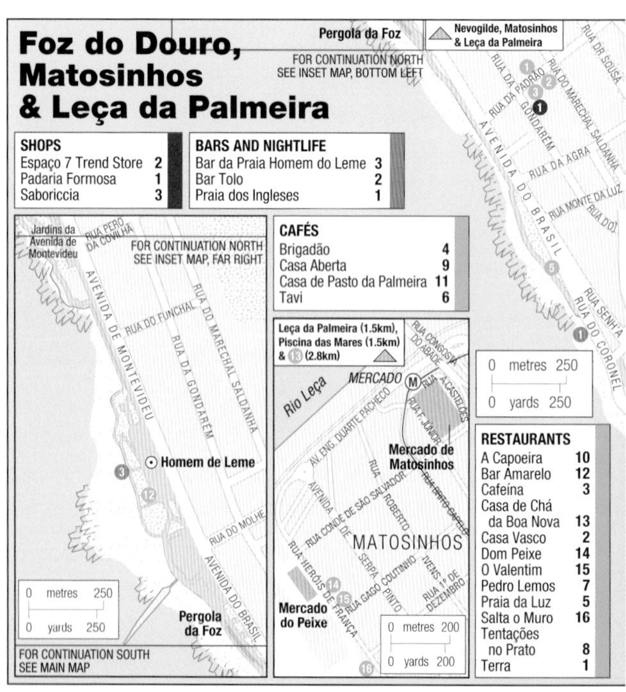

Tues–Fri 1–5pm, Sat & Sun 11am–5pm; May–Sept closes at 5.30pm. 50c.

At the northern end of Foz's seafront is the large roundabout of Praça do Gonçalves Zarco, where you'll find the austere **Castelo de Queijo** (Cheese castle). Officially called the Forte de São Francisco Xavier, it was given its nickname because the rock it was built on resembles a giant cheese. The fort was built in 1661 to protect Porto's coastline from North African pirates, though was pressed into action in the 1830s when it was besieged by Dom Pedro's troops during the Portuguese civil war. Today, it houses a tiny military museum dedicated to Portugal's veterans who saw action in the former colonies of Angola and Mozambique, plus an exhibition space for displays of ceramics and paintings. It's all very low-key, however – the real draw is the sea views from the battlements above.

Sea Life Porto

MAP p.92

1ª Rua Particular do Castelo do Queijo
226 190 400, visitsealife.com/porto.
Mid-July to Aug Mon–Fri 10am–6pm, Sat & Sun 10am–8pm; Sept to mid-July Mon–Fri 10am–6pm, Sat & Sun 10am–7pm. €13, online price €11; children under 12 €9, online price €8.

Part of the Sea Life franchise, this **aquarium** makes a fun excursion, with sharks, rays, jellyfish, starfish and thousands of other creatures. Many of the tanks reflect the different ecosystems; there's one on the Douro rRver, which is home to freshwater species, plus a tropical bay of rays and an exhibit of giant spider crabs and lobsters. There are exotic species from Portugal's Atlantic islands, the Azores, plus an underwater tunnel through a tank where sharks and Mariza the turtle live. There are regular feeding times accompanied by informative talks.

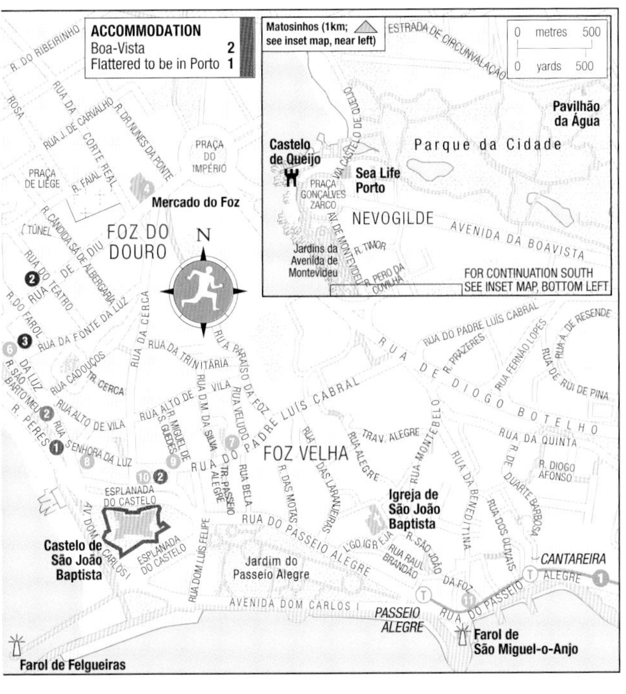

Architecture and the Porto School

Long known for its innovative building design (see box, p.51), Porto saw the emergence of its own style of contemporary architecture, with the so-called **Porto School** in the 1950s, centred on the city's School of Fine Arts. The Porto School proved fertile ground for many of the city's contemporary architects, including **Alcino Soutinho** (1930–2013), who worked on the conversion of the Casa-Museu Guerra Junqueiro (see p.37), and Amarante's Museu Amadeo de Souza-Cardoso (see p.109) and – most famously – local boy **Álvaro Siza Vieira** (born 1933), whose masterpiece in Porto is the contemporary art museum at the Fundação Serralves, which opened in 1999 (see p.87). Earlier works by Siza Vieira can be seen in Leça da Palmeira, at the sublime sea pools and at the *Casa de Chá da Boa Nova* restaurant (see p.97), which was built in 1963. Siza Vieira won the Pritzker Prize (architecture's equivalent of the Oscars) in 1992, and his equally influential protégé, **Eduardo Souto Moura** (born 1952), followed suit and won it in 2011. Perhaps best known for his work on the remarkable football stadium at Braga, Souto Moura has also worked in his hometown of Porto at the Casa das Artes, and on the renovation of the city's Museu dos Transportes e Comunicações (see p.72).

Foz de Douro has become something of a hotspot for architecture, with both Souto Moura and his mentor Siza Vieira living in the town – indeed, architecture buffs can admire Souto Moura's skills close up, by staying in a house he designed in 2005, which is tucked away down Rua Padre Luís Cabral: it's available to let through Ⓦ themodernhouse.com.

Parque de Cidade

MAP p.92

Entrance on Av da Boavista Ⓣ 225 320 080. Free.

Spreading inland from the seafront, the expansive **Parque de Cidade** is the largest urban park in Portugal, at just under a square kilometre. The park was opened in 2002, and today is peppered with paths that wend their way through lawned and wooded areas past four small lakes. Unsurprisingly it's a popular spot for weekend picnics – come on a weekday and it feels far removed from the bustle of the city. There's also a garden centre here (located in the southwest corner), as well as farm buildings (in the northeast corner) with a Centre for Environmental Education and weekend activities for children.

Pavilhão da Água

MAP p.92

Estrada da Circunvalação 15433 Ⓣ 226 151 820 Ⓦ pavilhaodaagua.com.

The shoe-box-like **Pavilhão da Água** (water pavilion) in the northeast section of the Parque da Cidade was built for the Lisbon Expo of 1998, but was moved here in the early 2000s. Although closed at the time of writing for renovation (check opening hours on website when it reopens), the Pavilhão da Água usually hosts imaginative displays and exhibits geared around the phases of the water cycle and their impact on the environment.

Piscinas das Mares

Matosinhos

Rua Heróis de França

Matosinhos' main claim to fame is as home to some of the region's finest fish and seafood restaurants, which cluster along Rua Heróis de França in the old quarter facing the fish market. Despite the earthy appearance of the street, people come for miles to dine here on top-quality fresh fish at reasonable prices (see p.97).

Mercado dos Matosinhos

MAP p.92

Rua França Júnior ⓣ 229 376 577. Mon 7am–2pm, Tues–Fri 6.30am–6pm, Sat 6.30am–1pm. Free. Ⓜ Mercado.

Matosinhos's **market** is one of the region's largest, set on two levels in a huge modern building with an impressive arched roof. Unsurprisingly, fish is the big thing here, with an astonishing array of sea creatures on sale, both familiar and bizarre. On the upper floor, you can find everything from fruit and vegetables, cakes and pastries, to caged rabbits and chickens.

Leça da Palmeira

Piscina das Mares

MAP p.92

Av da Liberade, Leça da Palmeira ⓣ 229 952 610, ⓦ matosinhosport.com. June–Sept daily 9am–7pm. Sat & Sun €8, or €5 for a half-day; Mon–Fri €6, or €4 for a half-day.

The highlight of Leça da Palmeira lies at the northern end of its the beach, the enticing **Piscina das Mares** (sea pools – with a separate one for kids) – neatly carved out of the rocks beside the ocean. Opened in 1966, they were designed by local architect Álvaro Siza Vieira (see box, opposite), who was also responsible for the sleek *Casa de Chá da Boa Nova* (see p. 97), another 2km up the seafront, one of the area's top restaurants.

Getting to Matosinhos

Matosinhos is on the blue **metro** line, with Brito Capelo the closest stop to the fish restaurants. Alternatively, take **bus** #500 from São Bento, which runs via the Foz do Douro seafront to Matosinhos market; or bus #502 from Bolhão to Parque de Cidade and Matosinhos.

Shops

Espaço 7 Trend Store

MAP p.92, POCKET MAP A12
Rua do Teatro 133, Foz do Douro
226 101 839. Mon–Sat 10.30am–7.30pm.

A renovated sixteenth-century house that is now home to several different boutiques selling clothes, bags, hats and furniture. There's also a simple basement café with a small outdoor patio, where you can get a decent brunch for €12.

Padaria Formosa

MAP p.92, POCKET MAP A12
Rua de Gondarém 362, Foz do Douro
226 180 781, padariaformosa.com. Mon–Thurs 7am–7pm, Fri 7am–7.30pm, Sat 7am–5pm, Sun 8am–1pm.

This attractive, tiled-floor building houses one of Porto's oldest bakeries, dating from 1898. It still sells home-made bread cooked in a wood oven, as well as some great cakes, pastries, biscuits and pies.

Saboriccia

MAP p.92, POCKET MAP A12
Rua Senhora da Luz 338–342, Foz do Douro
220 996 677. Mon–Sat 10am–7.30pm.

This little deli specializes in selling local produce from smallholders around Portugal, and is a great place to pick up wine, olive oil, jams, honey, cheeses and sweets.

Cafés

Brigadão

MAP p.92, POCKET MAP B12
Mercado do Foz, Rua de Diu, Foz do Douro
226 103 164, brigadao.pt. Mon–Fri 7am–7pm, Sat 7am–5pm.

Tiny café/shop selling home-made traditional *brigadeiros* – small, truffle-like sweets made from condensed milk in a variety of flavours, including passion fruit, port, dark chocolate and churros (€1.20 each). If one is not enough, you can buy a box to take-away.

Casa Aberta

MAP p.92, POCKET MAP B13
Rua Padre Luís Cabral 1080, Foz do Douro
226 170 271. Tues–Fri 10am–7.30pm, Sat 11am–7.30pm.

With a bike hanging from the ceiling and a Vespa as part of the decor, this is typical of Foz's hip spaces: it's part boutique shop – selling toys, clothes and crafts – and part café, selling moderately priced salads, sandwiches, scones and toasties from €5. There's a small terrace at the back.

Casa de Pasto da Palmeira

MAP p.92, POCKET MAP C13
Rua do Passeio Alegre 450, Foz do Douro
226 168 244. Daily noon–midnight.

Fashionable café-restaurant with outdoor tables facing the tram tracks and the Douro estuary. It's cosy inside too, and good for a range of teas, sharing plates, burgers and tapas (€4–10), though the menu changes monthly. Expect the likes of pork cheeks, *alheira* sausage or roasted octopus.

Tavi

MAP p.92, POCKET MAP A12
Rua da Senhora da Luz 363, Foz do Douro
226 180 152. Daily 8.30am–8pm.

Foz's best café is always busy thanks to its wonderful sea-facing terrace and counter full of amazing cakes and pastries. A smaller branch opposite is better for snacky sit-down meals (sandwiches and pizzas from €4–6).

Restaurants

A Capoeira

MAP p.92, POCKET MAP B13
Esplanada do Castelo 63, Foz do Douro
226 181 589. Mon–Sat 12.30–2.30pm & 8–11pm.

In a lovely tiled building, this place serves reliable, traditional Portuguese dishes: fresh hake and sole cost around €14, grilled turkey, veal or liver go for around

€9 and a variety of steaks from €14. It's popular with locals, so get there early to bag a table.

Bar Amarelo

MAP p.92
Av Montevideu, Homen de Leme, Foz do Douro ⓣ 226 182 963. Tues–Sun: June–Aug 11am–midnight; Sept–May 11am–6pm.

Basic, local fish restaurant right on the beach serving traditional dishes in a simple dining room overlooking the sea, or on the large outdoor terrace – the likes of fresh grilled sardines with tomato rice (€6.50) and grilled sea bass (€9.50) are usually on the menu.

Cafeína

MAP p.92, POCKET MAP A12
Rua do Padrão 100, Foz do Douro
ⓣ 226 108 059, ⓦ cafeina.pt. Mon–Thurs 12.30–6pm & 7.30pm–midnight, Fri–Sun 12.30–6pm & 7.30pm–2am.

A beautiful traditional dining-room with wooden floors, book-shelves on the walls and a homely vibe. It serves Portuguese dishes with an international twist such as cod gratin with onions (€19), or squid, mussel and prawn stew (€18). There's a good-value three-course lunch for €18 (€22 at weekends).

Casa de Chá da Boa Nova

MAP p.92
Av da Liberdade, Leça da Palmeira
ⓣ 229 940 066, ⓦ casadechadaboanova.pt. Mon 7.30–11pm, Tues–Sat 12.30–3pm & 7.30–11pm.

This stunning building, which seems to merge into the rocks that face the sea, was designed by Pritzer architect Ávaro Siza Vieria (see box, p.94) and is run by Michelin-starred chef Rui Paula (see p.57). As you'd expect, fish and seafood are the specialities, with a few à la carte dishes and a choice of three tasting menus: Earth and Sea (meat and fish) and Atlantic (fish and seafood) will set you back €125 (wine suggestions €85 extra), while the house menu

Casa de Chá da Boa Nova

is €90 (wine €45 extra) – all feature beautifully presented, innovative dishes. Reservations advised.

Casa Vasco

MAP p.92, POCKET MAP A12
Rua do Padrão 152, Foz do Douro
ⓣ 226 180 602, ⓦ casavasco.pt. Mon–Thurs & Sun 12.30–11pm; Fri & Sat 12.30pm–midnight.

A Scandi-style dining room, with grey wood walls and a pretty covered terrace with tables outside, the "Basque House" is a cosy, informal restaurant serving good food. There's a tapas-style menu during the afternoon (3.30–7.30pm), with more substantial dishes served at lunchtime and in the evening, such as fish cooked on the grill (€13), sea bass (€13) or seafood kebabs (€12.50).

Dom Peixe

MAP p.92
Rua Heróis de França, Matosinhos 241
ⓣ 224 927 160, ⓦ dompeixe.com. Daily noon–11pm.

One of the most highly rated of Matosinhos's fish restaurants, right opposite the fish market, this restaurant has a small outdoor terrace, slick service and a contemporary interior. Most fish is priced by the kilo: expect to pay around €8 for salmon, sardines or squid, around €11 for other fish.

O Valentim

MAP p.92
Rua Heróis de França, Matosinhos 263 ⓣ 229 388 015 ⓦ ovalentim.com. Daily noon–11pm.

With the same owners as *Dom Peixe* (see p.97), this is another fine Matosinhos fish restaurant. Fresh fish is cooked on an outside grill, with most mains around €11–18. Expect the likes of John Dory, *espetada de tamboril* (monkfish kebab) and *açorda de camarão* (prawns cooked in a garlicky bread sauce).

Pedro Lemos

MAP p.92, POCKET MAP B13
Rua do Padre Luís Cabral 974, Foz do Douro ⓣ 220 115 986, ⓦ pedrolemos.net. Tues–Sun 12.30–3pm & 7.30–11pm.

Tucked into an attractive backstreet of old Foz, this is a surprisingly small and cosy home for a Michelin Star restaurant run by one of the city's most illustrious chefs. You'll have to book in advance for its five- or seven-course tasting menu, which features changing dishes depending on what's in season: some of the herbs and vegetables come from the outdoor terrace garden, which also has alluring tables under the shade of umbrellas. Chef Pedro Lemos offers an original twist on largely local ingredients, and the menu may well feature the likes of chilled watermelon soup, tuna with asparagus, quail with mushrooms and sea bass with turnip and chestnuts. Everything is fresh and delicious, service is slick, and each dish can be paired with a fine wine, though you can expect to pay over €100 a head.

Terra

Praia da Luz

MAP p.92, POCKET MAP A12
Av do Brasil, Foz do Douro ⓣ 226 173 234, ⓦ praiadaluz.pt. Daily 10am–midnight.

Right on the sand and rock beach of the same name, this is a fab Foz chill-out spot, with lots of comfy chairs on terraces facing the waves, as well as tables inside a pavilion-type building. Considering its prime position, prices are surprisingly reasonable: fresh fish, grilled meats or pasta dishes start at €15, or you can easily ensconce yourself here with a drink or two to watch the sun set.

Salto o Muro

MAP p.92
Rua Heróis de França 386, Matosinhos ⓣ 229 380 870. Tues–Sat 12.15–3pm & 7.15–10.30pm.

The "Jump the Wall" is an engaging, if cramped, family-run *tasca* on the dockside Matosinhos street, which is full of fish restaurants. The other places might look more enticing, but stick with it – a handwritten menu offers the catch of the day, plus some home-style specials (such as *arroz de polvo* or baked sardines), and you'll get three courses, house wine and coffee for under €20.

Tentações no Prato

MAP p.92, POCKET MAP B13
Rua Senhora da Luz 97, Foz do Douro ⓣ 226 182 738. Tues–Sat noon–3pm & 7–10pm, Sun noon–3pm.

This attractive tiled restaurant is run by a team of dedicated women who rustle up a small but tasty array of dishes such as hake or octopus rice and *bacalhau* (around €10–13). The steak with beer sauce is recommended (€14.50). It's very popular, so reserve in advance.

Praia dos Ingleses

Terra

MAP p.92, POCKET MAP A12
Rua do Padrão 103, Foz do Douro
226 177 339, restauranteterra.com.
Daily noon–4pm & 8pm–midnight.

Hip and very popular restaurant in an attractive tiled building covered in geometric designs. Inside, there are lots of exposed wood beams and tables on two floors of a surprisingly spacious restaurant, and the menu also springs a few surprises: along with the usual Portuguese grilled meat and fish, you'll find pasta dishes, risotto and even sushi, all cooked to a high standard. Mains from around €15.

Bars and clubs

Bar da Praia Homem do Leme

MAP p.92
Av Montevideu 88, Foz do Douro 226 181 847. Daily: Sept–May 9am–7pm; June–Aug 9am–late.

Modern bar-café pretty much on the beach, with fantastic views through huge glass windows and from the terrace in front. It serves drinks, snacks, salads (€10) and sandwiches (€6).

Bar Tolo

MAP p.92, POCKET MAP A13
Rua Senhora da Luz 185, Foz do Douro
224 938 987. Mon–Wed & Sun 12.30pm–midnight, Thurs–Sat noon–2am.

This tall, friendly café-bar on three floors serves tapas (around €5–7) and a few daily specials (€8–10). It can be a bit smoky on the ground floor so head up to the pretty roof terrace on the top floor with views over the sea, or sit outside on the ground-floor patio.

Praia dos Ingleses

MAP p.92, POCKET MAP A12
Rua Coronel Raúl Peres, Foz do Douro
226 170 419, praiadosingleses.pt.
Daily 10am–2am.

An alluring beachside café-bar with a sea-facing terrace – waves crash right up to the terrace at high tide – comfy chairs and beanbags plus jazzy sounds. There's a long list of cocktails and sangrias to sample from €6, as well as fruit teas and various snacks including scones, croissants and cheese *tostas* (all under €3). There's also more substantial options of salads, crepes and grills (around €6–9). As the evening progresses, there's often a late-night DJ.

Vila do Conde

To sample northern Portugal's beaches at their best, it is worth taking the swift metro ride up the coast to Vila do Conde. Set slightly inland on the river Ave, it's a historic town which grew up as an important ship-building centre, peered over by the majestic Convento de Santa Clara. Along with a ship-building museum, there's also an engaging embroidery museum boasting the world's largest piece of lace. Despite the old town attractions, however, it is the nearby beach, a fine swathe of soft golden sands, which pulls in most visitors.

The old town

Vila do Conde's old town clusters round the north bank of the Rio Ave, its riverfront lined with appealing cafés and restaurants. Anchoring the old town's cobbled alleys is the beautiful Manueline **Igreja Matriz** (daily 10am–noon & 3–7.30pm), with its impressive carved and gilded altar and tiled chapel. Begun in the late fifteenth century, the church was designed by João de Castilho, who was also responsible for Seville's cathedral. In 1845, Portugal's greatest realist author, Eça de Queiroz was baptized in the church. Nearby, the Friday **market** (9am–6pm) takes place, where you'll find everything from farm produce to traditional children's toys.

Convento de Santa Clara

MAP p.102

Largo Dom Afonso Sanches. No public access.

The grand seventeenth-century **Convento de Santa Clara** is Vila do Conde's major landmark. Built to replace an earlier fourteenth-century monastery, the convent sits high above the old bridge and, while it's not open to the public, it is worth climbing up to the *miradouro* for sweeping views of the town and river. Running directly into the north side of the convent is a well-preserved, early eighteenth-century **aqueduct** which once carried water over a reputed 999 arches from Terroso, 5km north of town – the metro line to

Convento de Santa Clara

Getting to Vila do Conde

The easiest way to get to Vila do Conde from Porto is to take **metro** Line B. The stopping trains (1hr) call at Santa Clara, 300m east of the old town, and Vila do Conde, the same distance north of the old town. These alternate with faster Express trains (50min, marked Exp), which only call at Vila do Conde. There are four trains an hour (Mon–Fri), two–three an hour at weekends. You need a Zone 6 Andante card to travel this far (total, with card, €6.10 return).

Póvoa do Varzim now cuts right through part of the remaining course. The other thing worth noting about the convent is its long tradition of pastry-making – the so-called *doces conventuais*, or convent cakes (see box, p.103), sickly sweet affairs that generally involve industrial quantities of sugar and eggs, and are now available in cafés and *patisseries* all over the town.

Museu de Rendas de Bilros

MAP p.102
Rua de São Bento 70 ⓣ 252 248 470, ⓦ www.cm-viladoconde.pt. Tues–Sun 10am–noon & 2–6pm. €1.07.

The town of Vila do Conde is also known for its traditional lacework and embroidery (*rendas de bilros*), and there is an active lacework school in the interesting **Museu de Rendas de Bilros**, which is housed in one of the town's old manor houses. *Rendilheiras* (lace-makers) show off their skills here most days, surrounded by lovely examples of lacework and historic lace-making tools and equipment. Pride of place goes to what is officially the largest piece of lace in the world, which was made here by 150 lace-makers in 2015. The piece consists of 440 squares of lace, each of which measure 30cm x 30cm. The museum is also a good place to buy lace, and you'll see more for sale in the market and in shops around the town.

Museu da Construção Naval

MAP p.102
Largo da Alfândega ⓣ 252 617 506. Tues–Sun 10am–6pm. €1.10, includes entry to Nau Quinhentista.

Vila do Conde's shipbuilding industry is among the oldest in Europe, and fishing boats reminiscent of fifteenth-century caravels are still constructed here, in the shipyards on the other side of the river. You can trace this heritage in the excellent **Museu da Construção Naval**, which is housed in the impressive former royal customs house, the Alfândega Régia (1487), located down by the riverfront. Inside, you can see waxwork figures of the former customs' men and smugglers and find information about the old customs house; there's also an exhibition on the history of ships since the seventeenth century with models and photos.

Nau Quinhentista

MAP p.102
Largo da Alfândega ⓣ 252 248 400. Tues–Sun 10am–6pm. €1.10, includes entry to Museu da Construção Naval.

Right on the riverfront is a replica of a sixteenth-century sailing vessel, which you can visit and get an idea of what it was like to live and work on a boat which once transported cargo from India. During the months at sea, the cramped ship would have been stuffed with supplies to keep the crew going.

Vila do Conde festivals

A good time to visit Vila do Conde is for the nine-day food fair **Feira de Gastronomia** (gastronomia.vconde.org), which takes place in the third week in August. There are around sixty stands set up in Jardim da Avenida Júlio Graça selling produce from around the country, from cakes and traditional pastries to olives, cheeses, pies and local liqueurs.

The same location also hosts the oldest craft fair in the country, the renowned **Feira Nacional de Artesanato** (fna.vconde.org). From the last week of July to the first week of August, you can see craftsmen selling their produce, including everything from baskets to lace and Portuguese guitars. People also come from far and wide for **Curtas** (curtas.pt), the European short-film festival held here for a week every July.

Casa do Barco

MAP p.102

Rua do Cais da Alfândega 252 248 445. Daily: April to mid-Sept 9am–7pm, mid-Sept to May 9am–6pm. Free.

The modern glass pavilion on the riverfront doubles as a regional tourist information office and a shop, with a small exhibition detailing the history of fishing.

Capela do Socorro

MAP p.102

Rua do Socorro. No set opening hours.

You can't miss the distinctive white Moorish dome of the

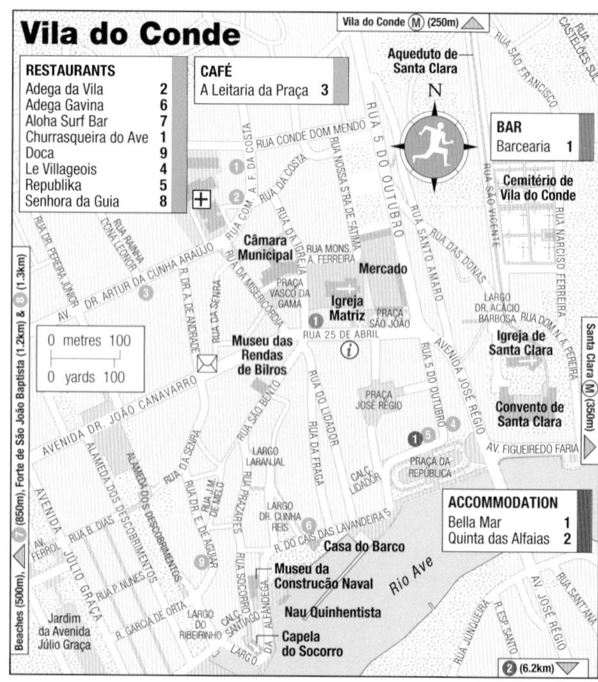

The beach at Vila do Conde

sixteenth-century **Capela do Socorro** that stands overlooking the riverside. Built in 1559 by Gaspar Manuel, a sailor and member of the Order of Christ, this unusual little chapel is completely round, and deceptively very plain from the outside. Its interior, however, is lined with impressive blue *azulejos* that depict scenes from the life of Christ, and are interrupted only by a vast wooden altar.

The beach

MAP p.102

The **beach** is a good fifteen-minute walk west of the town centre, and boasts long stretches of wave-battered sands that are just perfect for a lazy afternoon – though be aware that the Atlantic can be cold (and rough) even in August. To the south, the sands come to an end at the mouth of the Rio Ave, marked by the stumpy seventeenth-century Forte de São João Baptista.

Convent sweets

Portugal's tradition of **sweets and cakes** dates back to the fifteenth and sixteenth centuries, when traders started to import sugar from plantations in the Portuguese colonies. It was an expensive commodity and the Church was one of the few institutions that could afford to buy it. As a result, convents began to develop recipes for what became known as *doces conventuais*, or convent sweets, which they sold to make extra funds for Church coffers. The recipes often used sugar and egg yolks (the egg whites were used to starch the nuns' habits) and the resulting cakes were given slightly risqué names such as *Colchão de Noiva* (Bride's Mattress) and *Papos de Anjo* (Angel's Throats). The sweets are still made today using the traditional recipes, so if you want to sink your teeth into a *Barriga de Freira* (Nun's Belly), you can probably find one at the nearest *pastelaria*.

Ageda da Vila

Café

A Leitaria da Praça

MAP p.102
Av Dr Artur Cunha Araujo 123 ⓣ 224 036 244. Mon–Fri 9am–7pm.

This attractive café and bakery is right by the market building and serves a good range of cakes and pastries from a couple of euros, as well as fresh bread. There are also tables outside on the pretty square.

Restaurants

Adega da Vila

MAP p.102
Rua Comendador António Fernandes da Costa 57 ⓣ 961 258 237. Daily 8pm–midnight.

Traditional brick-lined restaurant with bottles and hams hanging from the wall, wooden tables and a few stools at the bar. It serves authentic local tapas dishes (€4–7), such as octopus with green sauce, or a plate of clams, and you can chose tasty accompaniments such as wild rice. It's tiny, so you'll need to book.

Adega Gavina

MAP p.102
Cais das Lavandeiras 56 ⓣ 917 834 517. Tues–Sun noon–3.30pm & 7.30–11pm.

Freshly caught fish and seafood are all cooked outside on the barbecue at this friendly restaurant with a cosy, traditional interior and tables outside overlooking the river. The menu varies depending on what has been caught, but you can expect the likes of a large sea bass for two people (€35) or octopus and tiger prawns grilled on the barbecue (both €15), and washed down with a jug of fruity house wine.

Aloha Surf Bar

MAP p.102
Av Manuel Barros ⓣ 252 618 886. Tues–Thurs 9am–7pm, Fri, Sat & Sun 9am–midnight.

A lovely location right on the seafront with comfy chairs and tables on the terrace, where you can watch the waves breaking on the beach below. It's smart, with contemporary decor inside, and charges surprisingly reasonable prices given its prime position. The menu features a selection of tapas-style dishes – you can settle in to watch the sunset with eight prawns and a small beer for just €6.50, or a platter of hams for €5. Larger dishes are good value too, such as *frango na brasa* (€7.50) or a mixed meat grill (€8), both served with chips, rice and salad, while the set lunch is top value at €6.50 for soup, a fish dish, drink, bread and coffee. The attached Aloha Surf and SUP school (ⓦ alohasurfsup.com) takes out paddle-boarding and surf groups and provides lessons.

Churrasqueira do Ave

MAP p.102

Rua Comendador António Fernandes da Coasta 95 ⓣ 252 633 391. Tues–Sun 11am–11pm.

Simple, but serving up good food, this modern grill house has a few tables outside which fill with locals who come here for the barbecued dishes such as *frango* on the grill (€7), a huge mixed meat grill (€20 for two people sharing) or half a barbecued rabbit. If you fancy something lighter than a grill then they also serve plates of black pork ham and cheese.

Doca

MAP p.102

Rua Dr Elias de Aguiar 35/Largo do Ribeirinho 5 ⓣ 252 642 106. Tues–Sun noon–3pm & 7.30–11pm.

With a smart interior, this restaurant is very popular with the townsfolk for its tasty local dishes, such as *arroz de tamboril* (monkfish rice) and roast goat (€30 for two people). The hearty lunch dish-of-the-day is excellent value at €7 for soup and a main, which might include the *bacalau com natas* (cod cooked in cream), plus pudding or coffee.

Doca

Le Villageois

MAP p.102

Praça da República 94 ⓣ 252 631 119. Tues–Sun noon–3pm & 7–10.30pm.

With its attractive tiled interior and tables and chairs outside on the riverfront, this well-regarded restaurant specializes in fish dishes, such as grilled sea bass (€11), squid and prawn kebabs, or *filletes de pescada* (€8).

Republika

MAP p.102

Praça da República ⓣ 252 696 373. Mon–Sat noon–3pm & 7–10pm.

Upmarket restaurant and tapas bar facing the river, with a varied menu featuring well-prepared meat and fish: steaks, grilled octopus and sumptuous tiger prawns. Expect to pay €30 upwards.

Senhora da Guia

MAP p.102

Av do Brasil ⓣ 968 518 835. Daily 9am–10pm; food served 12.30–3pm & 7.30–10.30pm.

Right on the beach, beside the Forte de São João Baptista, this basic beach café is a perfect sunset spot – though service can be slow. Fresh fish is cooked at lunch and dinner on the outside grill – squid kebab (€9), sardines (€8) or sea bass (€10) – while sandwiches and *tostas* are served all day (from €2).

Bar

Barcearia

MAP p.102

1 Piso, Rua da Igreja 8 ⓣ 252 170 114. Daily 8.30am–2am.

Lively, popular bar/*cervejaria* with a nice outdoor garden and covered terrace. It serves a variety of fresh juices (€3), milkshakes (€2.50) and simple food such as sandwiches, salad and mushroom *tostas* (€3.50) – and stays open till late.

Amarante

The small town of Amarante provides a taste of the best of rural northern Portugal, and makes for an appealing break from the bustle of Porto. The town is a delightful medley of tall handsome houses set either side of the Rio Tâmega, crossed by a picturesque arched stone bridge, the Ponte de São Gonçalo. Amarante's attractions include a bustling Wednesday and Saturday market, two impressive churches and a museum dedicated to the town's most famous artist, Amadeo de Souza-Cardoso. Throw in one of the country's top restaurants, and the pleasant hour's journey from Porto through rolling verdant countryside makes it well worth a day-trip.

The old town

Although modern Amarante looks relatively sizeable on its approach (it has a population of around 56,000), spreading up the slopes of the surrounding hills, its quaint **old town** nestles either side of the gently flowing Rio Tâmega, a tributary of the Douro and can easily be explored in a morning or afternoon. However, with one of the top hotels in the region (see p.118) and Michelin-starred restaurant *Largo do Paço* (see p.110), you might well be tempted to stay the night. The **market days** (Wednesday and Saturday 8am–3pm) are the liveliest, with fruit, veg and flower stalls filling the indoor market building, while traders selling cheap clothes, bags and traditional hats spill out onto the square outside. As the evening approaches, the local hooch, Gatão, a fruity *vinho verde*, can be enjoyed at one of the few late-opening esplanade bars found on the south side of the river near either of the town's bridges.

Ponte de São Gonçalo

Ponte de São Gonçalo

The **Ponte de São Gonçalo**, the handsome arched bridge over the river Tâmega, dates back to the eighteenth century when it replaced an original structure that was said to have been built largely by hand by São Gonçalo (see box, p.108). The original bridge was destroyed after a flood in 1763.

The current bridge of Ponte de São Gonçalo played a prominent role in the Napoleonic Wars, when in 1809, Portuguese soldiers heroically used the

Getting to Amarante

The trip by bus (or car) from Porto to Amarante – which lies 60km away – takes less than an hour via the A4. Once you've cleared Porto's sprawling suburbs, the journey is an attractive one taking you through bucolic rolling countryside and winding valleys that are lined with stepped terraces of vineyards. Regular Rodonorte services depart from Porto's Garagem Atlântico, which is located on Rua Alexandre Herculano near Praça da Batalha. The 9am Rodonorte service, returning at 3.30pm, makes for an ideal day-trip (see Ⓦrodonorte.pt for more details). In Amarante, the bus station is on Rua António Carneiro, which is a five-minute walk south of the river.

river here to resist an invasion by French troops. At the time, the French army had captured Porto, but were unable to cross the Tâmega at Amarante to link up with their troops in Spain because the Portuguese had mined the bridge. The Portuguese troops held out for fourteen days, until the French army took advantage of the gloom provided by a foggy morning to disarm the fuse mechanism, and finally stormed the bridge. Taken by surprise, the Portuguese army fled in panic, but they had delayed the French long enough for Wellington's British troops to reach Lisbon, a move which eventually tipped the balance of power away from Napoleon's men.

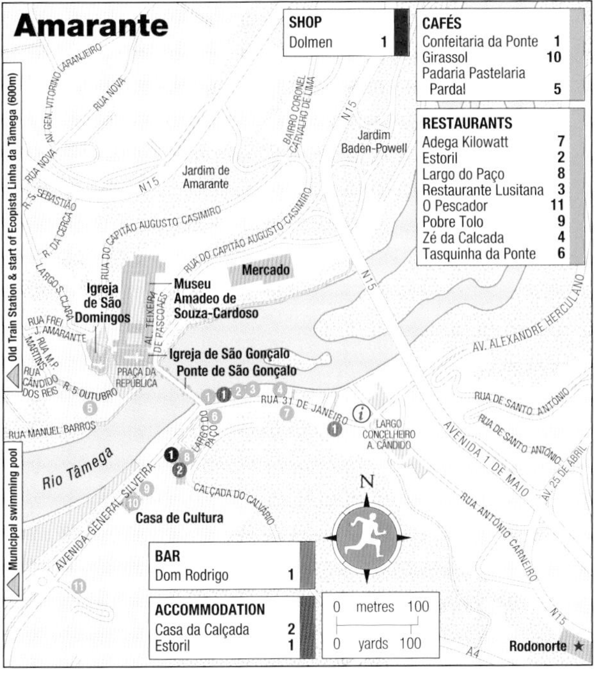

Gonçalo the hermit

The thirteenth-century saint, **São Gonçalo** was born into a wealthy family, before deciding to become a priest and embark on a fourteen-year pilgrimage to the holy lands, during which time he left his nephew to guard his estate. Gonçalo's travels persuaded him to renounce worldly goods, and he looked so impoverished on his return that his nephew is said to have set dogs on him to chase him away. Gonçalo then decided to live as a hermit and build a bridge over the Tâmega, largely with his own hands. Soon, he began to perform miracles: when the labourers who were helping him with the construction ran out of wine, he is said to have hit a rock with a stick, after which wine flowed from under it. He is also said to have summoned fish out of the river for the workers to eat. Gonçalo subsequently became the town's patron saint, and after his death, Amarante became a destination for pilgrims. The saint's annual festival – known as the **Festas do Junho** – is celebrated over the first weekend in June, with the belief that Gonçalo's lasting miraculous powers can help find people a partner. This belief has also led to the traditional exchange of phallic cakes by unmarried couples.

Igreja de São Gonçalo

MAP p.107

Praça da República. Daily 8am–7pm. Free.

Cross the old stone Ponte de São Gonçalo over the Tâmega and you're confronted by the landmark **Igreja de São Gonçalo**, the most important church in Amarante. Construction started in 1540 under the reign of João III, on the spot where Gonçalo's hermitage once stood, although the holy site almost certainly dates back to pagan times. It took over fifty years and three more royals before construction of the church was complete: the facade features the Varanda dos Reis, displaying statues of the founding monarchs João III, Sebastião, Henrique and Felipe I. Inside the church, touching the saint's well-worn tomb allegedly brings forward the happy wedding day for hitherto thwarted lovers.

Painting of São Gonçalo

Museu Amadeo de Souza-Cardoso

MAP p.107

Alameda Teixeira de Pascoaes ⓣ 255 420 272, ⓦ amadeosouza-cardoso.pt. June–Sept Tues–Sun 10am–12.30pm & 2–6pm; Oct–May Tues–Sun 9.30am–12.30pm & 2–5.30pm; last entry 30min before closing. €1, under-15s free.

The remodelled Renaissance cloisters around the side of São Gonçalo church make an appealing backdrop for the **Museu Amadeo de Souza-Cardoso**, largely based around the Cubist and avant-garde works of Amadeo de Souza-Cardoso (1887–1918). Born and brought up in Amarante, he spent his formative years as an artist in Paris and Brussels, where he made friends with influential artists including Modigliani and Brancusi, and his works were exhibited in Germany and at the Armory Show in New York. He returned to Portugal, but died young in the influenza pandemic of 1918. He's still relatively little known outside Portugal, though a retrospective of his work was held in Paris in 2016. The absorbing collection in Amarante is well worth a look, his works using beautiful if muted colours. Look out for the intriguing *Water-mills* (1915) and the almost pixillated *Life of Instruments* (1915–16). There are also amusing caricatures such as the *Caricature of Emmérico Nunes* (1910). The museum features works by other artists, too, including the Amarante-born Expressionist António Carneiro (1872–1930). There are also temporary exhibitions.

Igreja de São Domingos

MAP p.107

Praça da República. Daily: June–Sept 3–7pm; Oct–May 3–5pm, though opening hours can vary. Free, museum €1.

A steep granite stairway climbs from Amarante's main square, past the eighteenth-century **Igreja de São Domingos**, whose bell-tower chimes the hours. Take a quick look inside the intimate chapel – by the door is an extraordinary carved wooden tablet showing Christ suspended upside down on the Cross, hoisted by three men operating a rope and pulley. The church also contains the small and mildly interesting Museu de Arte Sacra, with religious art from the sixteenth to the nineteenth century displayed across two floors.

Cycling along the Tâmega

In days gone by, the approach to Amarante was truly scenic, on the old Tâmega branch train line, with rattling wooden carriages snaking along a single-track route up the valley. Although long discontinued, part of the track now has a new lease of life as the **Ecopista da Linha do Tâmega**, a "green route" that's been opened from the old station at Amarante to that of Chapa, just over 9km to the northeast. In time, it's planned to extend the hiking and biking track as far as Celorico de Basto (22km from Amarante) and Arco de Baúlhe (40km), but even now, the shortish stretch to Chapa makes for a lovely day out, along the river valley, through pine and eucalyptus, over the occasional bridge and past abandoned buildings. You can hire bikes for €5.50 a day (or €3.25 a half-day) from the Casa Cultura at Avenida General Silveira 193 (ⓣ 255 420 234, ⓦ cm-amarante.pt).

Shop

Dolmen

MAP p.107
Av General Silveira 59 ⓣ 255 100 025, ⓦ dolmen.pt. Daily 9am–12.30pm & 2–7pm.

Upmarket shop selling pricey, but top-quality, local handicrafts, including hand-embroidered serviettes and tablecloths, local cheese, olive oil, wines and honey.

Cafés

Confeitaria da Ponte

MAP p.107
Rua 31 de Janeiro ⓣ 255 432 034, ⓦ confeitariadaponte.pt. Daily 8.30am–8pm.

The best place for coffee and cakes (under €4) is right by the bridge, with a lovely riverside terrace. The nuns of the (now ruined) Santa Clara convent once made the town's famous *doces*, and you can sample them here, including home-made *bolos de São Gonçalo* (saint's cakes) and *pão de ló* (sponge cake).

Girassol

MAP p.107
Casa Cultura, Av General Silveira 193 ⓣ 255 420 234, ⓦ cm-amarante.pt. Daily 8am–midnight.

Simple café in a youth centre with an attractive river terrace. It serves bargain vegetarian lunches for €5. In the evening, it turns into more of a bar and is popular with students.

Confeitaria da Ponte

Padaria Pastelaria Pardal

MAP p.107
Rua 5 Outubro 43 ⓣ 255 423 019. Daily 8am–7pm.

This pretty tiled *pastelaria* sells a great selection of cakes, breads and pastries to take away or eat here The light and airy dining room with views over the river at the back also makes a good lunch spot – or you can sit at the tables on the street in front – for a bowl of soup (€1.50) and a sandwich (€2.50), with freshly squeezed juices served in a jar.

Restaurants

Adega Kilowatt

MAP p.107
Rua 31 de Janeiro ⓣ 255 433 159. Tues–Sun 9am–7.30pm.

Tiny traditional restaurant that's been in business for over 80 years, with tiled walls and smoked hams hanging from the bar. Squeeze inside for a tapas plate for two of ham, sausage and cheese (€8.50). Sandwiches are a bargain €2.

Estoril

MAP p.107
Rua 31 de Janeiro 150–152 ⓣ 255 431 291. Daily noon–3pm & 7–10pm.

This simple restaurant has a back terrace boasting lovely river views, and is a tranquil spot for well-priced dishes such as local trout, sardines, grilled chicken and other grilled meats, all from around €7.

Largo do Paço

MAP p.107
Casa da Calcaola, Largo do Paço 6 ⓣ 255 410 830, ⓦ casadacalcada.com. Daily 12.30–3pm & 7.30–10.30pm.

Michelin-star chef André Silva does sublime things with local produce in a series of tasting menus (dinner from €55, lunch from €25). Expect a creative twist on tradition with a seasonal edge, which in autumn and winter might mean rabbit stuffed with pistachios and served with a mustard and herb crust or roast pigeon with sautéed cherries.

O Pescador

MAP p.107
Av General Silveira ☎ 255 422 004. Tues–Sun noon–11pm.

Just off the main riverside road, this quirky restaurant has two cosy, tucked-away dining rooms. Popular with locals, especially for lunch, it has a good-value menu with pork steaks, *picanha* (garlicky strips of beef) and grilled meats for around €6. There's fresh fish, too (€15).

Pobre Tolo

MAP p.107
Av General Silveira 169 ☎ 255 422 088, pobretolo.pt. Mon & Wed–Sun noon–3pm & 7–10pm.

Smart option on the riverfront road opposite the old town, serving regional cuisine: braised octopus, monkfish rice and chicken in puff pastry are all recommended, as are the desserts. Mains start at €25, but half portions should suffice. There's usually an inexpensive set lunch.

Restaurante Lusitana

MAP p.107
Rua 31 de Janeiro 65 ☎ 255 426 720. Mon, Wed, Thurs & Fri 11.30–2pm & 7–10pm, Tues 11.30am–2pm, Sat & Sun 11.30am–10pm.

Cosy place with tiled walls and a balcony overlooking the river. It serves good value dishes such as grilled salmon for €10, plus specialities of roast veal (€10) and *tripas à la moda da casa* (tripe).

Tasquinha da Ponte

MAP p.107
Rua 31 de Janeiro 193 ☎ 255 433 715. Mon & Wed–Sun 9am–midnight, Tues 9am–4pm.

Cosy downstairs place right by the Ponte de São Gonçalo serving simple good-quality home cooking at bargain prices – all dishes cost €5–9, and the menu may feature the likes of grilled chicken with chips and rice, bean and meat stew (€5) or sardines with green beans (€5).

Estoril

Zé da Calcada

MAP p.107
Rua 31 de Janeiro 83 ☎ 255 426 814, zedacalcada.com. Daily noon–3.30pm & 7–10.30pm.

The nicest of the riverside choices has a terrace with a river view and serves good regional food (dishes €10–18), farom *bacalhau* to *posta á Maronesa* (hefty steaks from the nearby Serra do Marão). The €9 buffet lunch (Mon–Fri noon–2.30pm) gets you a choice of hot and cold dishes including soup, coffee and a drink.

Bar

Dom Rodrigo

MAP p.107
Rua 31 de Janeiro 39 ☎ 919 318 042. Daily 9am–8pm.

The walls and tables of this tavern are smothered with messages from former satisfied customers, and it's easy to see why. Hams hang above the bar, and you can choose from these, smoked sausages or local cheeses, with a glass of wine for €5.

ACCOMMODATION

Pestana Palácio do Freixa

Hotels and guesthouses

Porto has been undergoing a tourism boom and has a wide range of accommodation to suit all budgets. Nevertheless, many places get booked up so it pays to reserve in advance. Nearly all the cheapest accommodation is in the city centre, while the boutique and smart accommodation tends to be in the medieval streets nearer the river. There are also good options in the upmarket suburbs of Boavista and out at the seaside in Foz do Douro: while the suburban location is a slight drawback, nowhere is much more than about thirty minutes' bus or metro ride from the centre. Only a few hotels have private parking, but some have cut-price deals with nearby car parks. There are also an increasing number of hostels (see page 119). Unless otherwise stated, all the prices quoted below are for the least expensive ensuite double room in high season, including breakfast.

Ribeira

1872 RIVER HOUSE MAP p.28, POCKET MAP D8. Rua do Infante Dom Henrique 133 ⓣ961 172 805, ⓦ1872riverhouse.com. A beautifully renovated, eight-roomed townhouse on the riverfront – the building sits partly on the old city walls, which you can see through the breakfast room's glass floor. Contemporary rooms but with lots of original features including stone walls and Art Deco tiles. The staff are super-helpful, and the excellent breakfasts are served in a room with river views. You can help yourself to free coffee, tea and beer during the day. It's worth paying the €50 extra for a riverview room, although the streetview ones are just as quaint. **€155**

Author picks

LUXURY *The Yeatman* p.116
BOUTIQUE *Flores Village* p.116
TRADITIONAL *Grande Hotel de Paris* p.116
BUDGET *Duas Nações* p.116
FAMILY-FRIENDLY *Flattered to be in Porto* p.118

CARRIS PORTO MAP p.28, POCKET MAP E7. Rua do Infante Dom Henrique 1 ⓣ808 145 5751, ⓦcarris-porto-ribeira.hotel-rn.com. A few steps up the hill from the city's waterside, this stylish four-star hotel has been carved out of five old buildings, creating a dramatic lobby space made up of soaring stone arches and cutaway floors. Handsome rooms feature hardwood floors, earth-toned fabrics and bathrooms, while breakfast is served in a restaurant that sits beneath huge granite arches and pillars. **€135**

DESCOBERTAS BOUTIQUE HOTEL MAP p.28, POCKET MAP E7. Rua Fonte Taurina 14, ⓣ222 011 471, ⓦdescobertasboutiquehotel.com. This comfortable boutique-style hotel is situated in a narrow cobbled street, just one block back from the riverfront. In a newly renovated old building, the eighteen rooms are comfortable and stylish and the decor, in a nod to the Portuguese Discoveries, has some ethnic touches. **€145**

GUEST HOUSE DOURO MAP p.28, POCKET MAP D8. Rua Fonte Taurina 99 ⓣ222 015 135, ⓦguesthousedouro.com. This super-cool waterfront B&B has windows right on the Douro. Not all the rooms have river views (some look over the medieval street outside instead), but there's a sharp sense of style throughout and you couldn't be closer to the action. There's also parking nearby. Closed early January. **€175**

INPATIO GUESTHOUSE MAP p.28, POCKET MAP D7. **Pátio de São Salvador 22, off Rua Mouzinho da Silveira 64 ⓣ 222 085 477, ⓦ inpatio.pt.** This renovated nineteenth-century house is tucked away in a tranquil patio: the comfortable, contemporary rooms are set over three floors, with kettles (something of a rarity in Portugal), bright white decor and grey slate bathrooms complete with Fair Trade toiletries. The superb breakfast features fresh local bread, pastries and cheeses as well as a different, though equally tasty, home-made cake served each day. **€110**

PESTANA VINTAGE PORTO MAP p.28, POCKET MAP E8. **Praça da Ribeira 1 ⓣ 223 402 300, ⓦ pestana.com.** Enjoying the Ribeira's best location, atop the medieval wall next to the river, this cluster of old buildings has been transformed into a boutique-style four-star hotel. Rooms are plush if not huge, and most face the Douro (corner rooms also overlook the Ponte de Dom Luís I bridge). **€190**

The Sé and Aliados

AMÉRICA MAP p.38, POCKET MAP H1. **Rua de Santa Catarina 1018 ⓣ 223 392 930, ⓦ hotel-america.net. ⓜ Faria Guimarães or Trindade.** Located in a slightly run-down area towards the top of Rua de Santa Catarina, the *América* is a well-regarded mid-range choice with bright and relatively spacious rooms, though there can be some street noise. There is also private underground parking and a bar. **€95**

CASTELO DE SANTA CATARINA MAP p.38. **Rua de Santa Catarina 1347 ⓣ 225 095 599, ⓦ castelosantacatarina.com.pt. ⓜ Faria Guimarães or Marquês or bus #701/#702/#703 from Mercado do Bolhão.** A 35min walk from the centre, this dramatic turreted folly was built at the end of the nineteenth century by a wealthy textiles merchant and now houses a modest guesthouse. The comfortable rooms aren't grand or expensive, but are furnished in period style, while breakfast is eaten in the lush *azulejo*-tiled gardens. There's parking, but no bar. **€82**

GRANDE HOTEL DO PORTO MAP p.38, POCKET MAP G4. **Rua de Santa Catarina 197 ⓣ 222 076 690, ⓦ grandehotelporto.com. ⓜ Bolhão.** Porto's oldest hotel (three stars) is steeped in nineteenth-century mercantile style, with polished marble and crystal chandeliers, and an echoing gilt-tinged restaurant where breakfast is served. It's in a handy location, on the main pedestrianized shopping street. Rooms are not huge but have contemporary decor, and prices are pretty good, especially during special promotions. There's limited parking, and a small gym. **€120**

NH COLLECTION MAP p.38, POCKET MAP G5. **Praça da Batalha 60–65 ⓣ 227 660 600. ⓦ nh-hotels.com. ⓜ São Bento.** A swanky modern hotel in a renovated eighteenth-century palace. It's perhaps a little corporate but it benefits from a great location. The rooms (and beds too) are spacious with flatscreen TVs, and some overlook the Praça de Batalha. There's also a range of good facilities including a gym, spa and indoor pool. Breakfast costs extra. **€190**

PESTANA PALÁCIO DO FREIXO MAP p.38. **Estrada Nacional 108 ⓣ 210 407 600, ⓦ pousadapalaciodofreixo.com. No metro or buses run here: a taxi into the town centre costs around €8.** A couple of kilometres east of the city centre in a majestic riverside location, is the magnificently restored Baroque *Palácio do Freixa*. Dating back to 1742, the main period-style building houses an elegant restaurant, bar and public rooms, while contemporary bedrooms – many with classic river views – are set in an adjacent former flour factory. There's an outdoor infinity pool with river views and you can also enjoy the indoor pool and spa. **€240**

Rooms with a view

1872 River House p.114
Guest House Douro p.114
Pestana Palácio do Freixo p.115
Boa-vista p.117
Pousada de Juventude p.119

The Baixa

DUAS NAÇÕES MAP p.49, POCKET MAP D4. Praça Guilherme Gomes Fernandes 59 **T** 222 081 616, **W** duasnacoes.com.pt. **M** Aliados. Don't be fooled by the run-down exterior, this budget gem has updated double-glazed rooms with satellite TV and central heating. It's popular with backpackers, as some bunk-style rooms sleep four with prices as low as €15/person. Double rooms are also offered: book ahead if you want a private bathroom. Breakfast is €1.50 extra. No credit cards. **€38**

FLORES VILLAGE MAP p.49, POCKET MAP E6. Rua das Flores 139 **T** 222 013 478, **W** floresvillage.com. **M** São Bento. On the fashionable, pedestrianized Rua das Flores, this boutique hotel is a clever conversion of an eighteenth-century townhouse, with five storeys at the front, and a hidden garden off the fourth floor at the back. The rooms are spacious and modern – those on the top floor have the best views over the city. There's even an atmospheric pool, secreted in the villa's former wine cellars, and full spa facilities, while a generous buffet breakfast is served in a grand room off the gardens. Good low-season deals. **€198**

GRANDE HOTEL DE PARIS MAP p.49, POCKET MAP E4. Rua da Fábrica 27–29 **T** 222 073 140, **W** hotelparis.pt. **M** Aliados. Opened in 1877, the *Grande Hotel de Paris* is more a guesthouse and has been frequented by Portugal's finest writers and artists, including Eça de Queiroz and poet Guerra Juncqueiro. The building retains many original fittings, with period furniture and high ceilings, a small garden and a good breakfast served in a splendid drawing room. Rear rooms have balconies and old-town views, and there are also interconnecting rooms for families (€150). **€90**

INFANTE SAGRES MAP p.49, POCKET MAP E4. Praça Dona Filipa de Lencastre 62 **T** 223 398 500, **W** hotelinfantesagres.pt. **M** Aliados. A glamorous, contemporary design hotel with antique Persian carpets, crystal chandeliers, Chinese porcelain and stained-glass windows which complement the funky Portuguese custom-made furniture and chic cosmopolitan style. There's an open-air patio, bar and good restaurant (called *Book*, in a former bookshop) and Asian-style spa, plus parking nearby. **€165**

PÃO DE AÇÚCAR MAP p.49, POCKET MAP E4. Rua do Almada 262 **T** 222 002 425, **W** paodeacucarhotel.pt. **M** Aliados. A fab Art Deco survivor from the 1940s that was once the favoured hotel of visiting artistes, including fado diva Amália Rodrigues. While the rooms could do with a style injection, they have shiny parquet floors and a fair amount of space. The best rooms (€150) on the top floor open onto a private terrace overlooking the town hall. The amazing spiral staircase also contains a collection of historic bumper cars, retrieved from a former fairground. **€140**

Vila Nova de Gaia

THE YEATMAN MAP p.p.49. Rua do Choupelo **T** 220 133 100, **W** the-yeatman-hotel.com. **M** General Torres. Porto's top hotel sits amid the historic port wine lodges, with fantastic views over the city and river from the gardens and all the rooms, many with spacious terraces. Both the infinity pools – one indoors with a luxurious spa, the other a decanter-shaped outdoor pool – have amazing panoramic views, too. The hotel is home to Portugal's top Michelin-starred restaurant (see p.70), and guests get a private tour with the sommelier of its wine cellar housing one of the world's best collections of Portuguese wines. Visiting football teams playing FC Porto often stay here, and one of the corridors displays a series of signed players' shirts, including Maradona and Ronaldo. Rates vary considerably throughout the year. **€315**

Miragaia and Masserelos

EUROSTAR DAS ARTES MAP p.49, POCKET MAP B3. Rua da Rosário 160–164 Ⓣ222 071 250, Ⓦwww.eurostarshotels.co.uk/eurostars-das-artes.html. ⓂAliados. The facade of a handsome tiled building in the heart of this fashionable district shelters a modern, contemporary hotel with rooms in two blocks – one for doubles and one for twin rooms. It's mostly geared towards business travellers, so is slightly anodyne, but the rooms are comfortable and there's a bar and small patio garden. **€120**

MERCADOR GUESTHOUSE MAP p.49, POCKET MAP B3. Rua Miguel Bombarda 382 Ⓣ911 059 755, Ⓦporto.mercador.com.pt. ⓂAliados or Trindade. On the arty Rua Miguel Bombarda, this attractive "Brazilian House" was built by a Portuguese merchant who made his fortune in the colony, and returned to Porto to show off his wealth. The house has been lovingly preserved in traditional style with seven comfortable rooms, and there's a pretty garden with a 100-year-old palm tree. **€90**

PORTA AZUL MAP p.49, POCKET MAP A4 & D10. Rua Dom Manuel II 204 Ⓣ224 037 706, Ⓦporta-azul.com. Bus #200 from Av Aliados. The "Blue Door" is a small, welcoming guesthouse right by the Jardim do Palácio de Cristal. Great value, it has just six rooms, most of which have a balcony overlooking, or direct access to, a pretty, sheltered garden. **€85**

ROSA ET AL TOWNHOUSE MAP p.49, POCKET MAP B3. Rua do Rosário 233 Ⓣ916 000 081, Ⓦrosaetal.pt. ⓂAliados or Trindade. Six boutique-style elegant suites occupy an impressively restored townhouse in an artsy, residential district near the Soares dos Reis museum. There's afternoon tea (served 4–6pm) and regular classes, such as the one on Portuguese gastronomy, which can be attended. All rooms come with hardwood floors, warm lighting and classy bathrooms with clawfooted baths, and some rooms have balconies. **€178**

VINCCI PORTO MAP p.49, POCKET MAP A10. Alameda de Basílio Teles 29 Ⓣ22 043 9620, Ⓦvincciporto.com. Tram #1 from Ribeira. Right on the riverfront, facing the Douro, this four-star hotel is in an imaginatively converted former fish market; breakfast is served in the high-ceilinged former main market area. Rooms are spacious and contemporary and there's also a bar, restaurant and free parking. **€150**

Boavista

CASA DO CONTO MAP p.84. Rua da Boavista 703 Ⓣ222 060 340, Ⓦcasadoconto.com. ⓂCarolina Michaelis. The *Casa do Conto* displays an impressive conversion of a nineteenth-century house into contemporary and architecturally interesting apartments, most with writing on the ceiling. Each apartment is slightly different but all are bright and spacious with kitchenettes and contemporary facilities, and the top-floor room comes with its own balcony. **€130**

HOTEL DA MÚSICA MAP p.84. Mercado do Bom Sucesso, Largo Ferreira Lapa 21 Ⓣ226 076 000, Ⓦhoteldamusica.com. ⓂCasa da Música. Located in the Bom Sucesso Market, and conveniently close to the Casa da Música (see p.86), this sleek design-hotel has 85 rooms spread across its four floors. The en-suite rooms are all musically themed and inspired by local and international composers. There's also a chic bar as well as a decent hotel restaurant. **€110**

Foz do Douro

BOA-VISTA MAP p.92, POCKET MAP B13. Esplanada do Castelo 58, Foz do Douro Ⓣ225 320 020, Ⓦhotelboavista.com. Tram #1 from Ribeira or bus #500 from São Bento. Ocean and river views are the thing at this traditional villa, set over the road from the fort at Foz do Douro – it's worth paying the extra €10 or so (and booking in advance) for a water-view room. A three-star establishment, the rooms are comfortable if unexceptional, but there's a fine rooftop pool and sun terrace, plus bar, restaurant and parking. **€100**

Vila do Conde

QUINTA DAS ALFAIAS MAP p.102. Rua da Trás 220, Fajozes, 10km southeast of town ⓣ252 662 146 or ⓣ919 900 509, ⓦquintadasalfaias.com. A wonderfully elegant nineteenth-century country house set in extensive gardens and orchards, with a pool and tennis court. It has four en-suite rooms with garden views, plus two suites (€110) and apartments sleeping four (€150) or six (€200) – the decor understated, with plenty of bare granite, and the style is traditional country-house. **€85**

Amarante

CASA DA CALÇADA MAP p.107. Largo do Paço 6 ⓣ255 410 830, ⓦcasadacalcada.com. This restored sixteenth-century palace is situated just above the bridge and is stuffed with objets d'art. It's set in magnificent gardens complete with pool, tennis court and even its own vineyard. The boutique-style rooms and suites vary in size, decor and outlook (not all have views), but all are extremely comfortable, and there's a Michelin-starred restaurant on site (see p.110). **€170**

ESTORIL MAP p.107. Rua 31 de Janeiro 49 ⓣ255 431 291. A star pick for budget travellers – pleasant, high-ceilinged en-suite rooms and, for a few euros more, a balcony overlooking the river and bridge. Breakfast isn't included, but the cheery attached restaurant is a firm favourite for inexpensive riverside terrace dining (see p.110). **€40**

Self-catering

There are some good options for self-catering in Porto, which often works out cheaper than a hotel, especially for groups or families. Along with the places listed below, try ⓦairbnb.co.uk or ⓦflatinporto.com.

BAUMHAUS MAP p.84. Rua da Boavista 781 ⓣ915 495 579, ⓦbaumhaus.pt/baumhaus. ⓜCarolina Michaelis. A nineteenth-century townhouse that has been newly renovated into nine self-catering apartments on five floors (one in the loft), each named after a Portuguese artist. The rooms have modern Scandi-style decor with all mod cons, and there's a lovely long garden with a barbecue area for the summer evenings. **Studios from €96**

FLATTERED TO BE IN PORTO MAP p.92, POCKET MAP A13. Rua Senhora da Luz 145 ⓣ939 146 262, ⓦflatteredapartments.com/porto. Light, airy, spacious apartments, some with fantastic sea views, in an old, beautifully renovated seaside house. The location is great – a stone's throw from both the beach and the cafés and restaurants of the old town. The apartments are modern, stylish and comfortable, with a well-equipped kitchenette, and the welcoming and helpful owner, Miguel, leaves a tasty breakfast basket outside the door each morning. Highly recommended. **€168**

THE PORTO RIVER APARTHOTEL MAP p.28, POCKET MAP E7. Rua dos Canastreiros 50 ⓣ223 401 210, ⓦportoriver.pt. In a great position, just back from the riverfront, this is a good option for self-caterers. The bright, white rooms (from studios to two-bed apartments) have small kitchenettes and bathrooms, though the price includes breakfast. It's worth paying the extra €20 or so for river views, as the back rooms overlook a narrow alley. **Studios from €185**

VITORIA VILLAGE MAP p.49, POCKET MAP D5. Rua das Flores 139 ⓣ220 013 477, ⓦfloresvillage.com. ⓜSão Bento. With a separate entrance on Rua da Vitoria and sharing all the facilities of the *Flores Village* (see p.116), the *Vitoria Village* offers spacious self-catering duplex apartments, some of which open directly onto the gardens. These are excellent for families, the largest sleeping up to six guests, with well-equipped kitchens. **€170**

Hostels

Porto's hostels have improved dramatically over the last few years, and many are chic and comfortable, with facilities on a par with (or better than) some hotels. Prices start at €15 for dorms and around €40 for a double room – about half the cost of the least expensive hotel. A youth hostel card is required for the official youth hostel (pousada da juventude) – you can buy one on your first night's stay. Unless stated, prices don't include breakfast.

BELLA MAR MAP p.102. **Praça da República 84 ⓣ 252 631 748. Ⓜ Santa Clara.** The *azulejo*-lined stone staircase leads to an excellent hostel with cosy, well-kept rooms sleeping two to four guests (with shared bathrooms). Don't expect up-to-the-minute decor and facilities, but the location by the main square is excellent. **€60**

BLUESOCK HOSTEL MAP p.28, POCKET MAP E7. **Rua de São João 40 ⓣ 227 664 171, ⓦ bluesockhostels.com. Ⓜ São Bento.** New hostel in a blue-tiled building, with traditional stone walls, wooden beams and modern facilities. The well-designed dorms (both mixed and female-only) have spacious bunks with charger points, lockers and curtains: there are also en-suite doubles and twins, plus a rooftop suite with breathtaking views. The friendly staff organize pub crawls and fado nights, and there's a lively bar in the vaulted cellar. Breakfast is included. **Dorms €20, doubles €99, suite €209**

PILOT DESIGN HOSTEL MAP p.49, POCKET MAP D3. **Largo Alberto Pimentel 11 ⓣ 222 084 362, ⓦ pilothostel.com. Ⓜ Trindade.** This friendly, funky hostel is in a good location close to one of the main bar areas, though it also has its own late-opening bar. It has various small but comfy dorms sleeping four to twelve guests, and there's a small back patio. It arranges various events including walking tours and pub crawls. **€20**

PORTO ALIVE MAP p.49, POCKET MAP E6. **Rua das Flores 138 ⓣ 220 937 693, ⓦ portoalivehostel.com. Ⓜ São Bento.** Well-located in a fashionable, pedestrianized street, this hostel has eight- or ten-bed dorms, which are contemporary though a bit small. There are double rooms too (with shared bathroom, including one with a balcony). There's a communal kitchen and living room. **Dorms €30, doubles €75,**

PORTO GALLERY HOSTEL MAP p.74, POCKET MAP B3. **Rua de Miguel Bombarda 222 ⓣ 224 964 313, ⓦ gallery-hostel .com. Ⓜ Aliados or Trinade.** In trendy Rua Miguel Bombarda, this renovated, family-run, 1906 townhouse has luxury en-suite four- and six-bed dorms plus double rooms. It hosts local artists' exhibitions, and the chill-out area has a small bar and living room with garden. **Dorms €20, doubles €70**

POUSADA DE JUVENTUDE MAP p.92. **Rua Paulo da Gama 551, Pasteleira, 4km west of the centre ⓣ 226 177 257, ⓦ pousadasjuventude .pt. Bus #504 from Ⓜ Casa da Música, or #500 from São Bento.** It's a bit of a way out, and not ideal for night owls, but most of the doubles and dorms in Porto's contemporary hostel have wonderful views of the Douro. There's also a self-contained apartment sleeping four. Book ahead in summer. **Dorms €15, doubles €40, apartment €70**

RIVOLI CINEMA HOSTEL MAP p.38, POCKET MAP F4. **Rua Dr Magalhães Lemos 83 ⓣ 220 174 634, ⓦ rivolicinemahostel. com. Ⓜ Aliados or Trindade.** Co-owned by a bunch of art-grad, movie-crazy friends, this bright, airy townhouse has film-themed dorms and double rooms, all sharing toilets and showers. It's funky and communal – one big breakfast table, a kitchen, lounge and outdoor roof terrace – and they organize events like poker nights and evening drinks. **Dorms €28, doubles €66**

ESSENTIALS

Metro crossing Ponte Dom Luís I

Arrival

Porto's airport is 13km north of the city and is well served by the metro and taxis. The city's train stations are connected to the metro while the various bus stations are all centrally located.

By air

Porto's **Francisco Sa Carneiro airport** (T 229 432 400, W ana.pt) is on Metro Line E (daily 6am–1am, every 20–30min; one-way travel ticket €1.95, plus a one-off cost of €0.60 for a rechargeable ticket), which takes you directly into the centre in around 30–45minutes – to Casa da Música (for Boavista hotels), Trindade, Aliados or Bolhão (for city-centre hotels), or São Bento or Campanhã (for onward train services). Taxis from the airport into the centre cost €20–30; make sure you get one from the authorized rank outside the terminal.

By train

Portugal's **trains** are run by CP (Comboio de Portugal T 707 210 220 W cp.pt). International, intercity and ALFA Pendular trains arrive at the **Estação de Campanhã**, 2km east of the city centre. With a ticket to Porto you can simply change here onto any local train for the central São Bento station, a five-minute ride away. Campanhã is also on the metro, or it's a €5 taxi ride into the centre. The **Estação de São Bento** is the city-centre station for suburban and regional services, and for connections to intercity and international services from Campanhã. There's a metro station here and taxis outside. You can buy tickets for any train at São Bento (even for Campanhã departures).

By bus

Buses to Porto arrive at various stops and garages all over the city, though most are fairly central. Eurolines (international services) use the **Internorte terminal** at Praça da Galiza (W internorte.pt, M Casa da Música). **Garagem Atlântico**, Rua Alexandre Herculano, near Praça da Batalha, is a hub for several companies including the national operator Rede Expressos (W www.rede-expressos.pt); Rodonorte (Estremadura, Ribatejo, Minho, Trás-os-Montes; W rodonorte.pt) and Santos (Beiras, Trás-os-Montes, Lisbon; W santosviagensturismo.pt) stop on Rua Ateneu Comercial, near Bolhão market; while Renex (Estremadura, Ribatejo, Lisbon, Algarve and Minho; W renex.pt) stop at Campo dos Mártires da Pátria 37, next to the Palácio da Justiça.

By car

Driving into Porto is to be avoided, if possible – the city centre is congested and the one-way system confusing. You don't need a car to see the city, so the best advice is to park where you can and use public transport. Major suburban metro stations have **parking** – particularly at the football stadium, Estádio do Dragão – or use one of the sign-posted city-centre car parks or garages; following signs for "Centro" or "Aliados" will send you into the maelstrom. Garage parking is expensive – around €2 per hour between 8am and 8pm, slightly cheaper overnight – but you'll have little choice if your hotel doesn't have parking, as on-street metered parking is limited to two hours (though it's free after 8pm and at weekends).

For **car rental**, most international companies have both downtown and airport offices; if you need a vehicle for exploring further afield it's far easier to pick up your car the day you leave Porto. Local companies include Auto-Jardim (W auto-jardim.com) and Guerin (W guerin.pt).

Getting around

You'll be able to walk – more like climb – between all the city-centre attractions, but you'll have to use public transport to get out to the Fundação Serralves museum, the coast and the airport. There's an extensive bus network, and a swift metro system, while a funicular and three vintage tram lines still remain in service. The local transport authority, STCP (808 200 166, www.stcp.pt), has a useful website (English version available), and information offices (Mon–Fri 8am–7.30pm, Sat 9am–12.30pm) in Campanhã train station and Casa da Música and Trindade metro stations. You can also take a **river taxi** (see box, p.61) between Ribeira and Vila Nova de Gaia, which docks near the Sandeman port wine lodge.

The metro

The modern **metro** system (metrodoporto.pt) runs on six lines, A to F, underground in the city centre and then overground to the airport and to suburban destinations. Hours of operation are daily from 6am to 1am (departures every 10–30min), and you need an Andante card (see box, p.124) to use the system.

Other than for the ride in from the airport, or for the trip up the coast to Matosinhos or Vila do Conde, the metro isn't particularly useful for sightseeing, though there are handy city-centre stops at Trindade, Aliados, Bolhão and São Bento, and you can also use it to go to the Casa da Música at the Rotunda da Boavista and FC Porto's stadium, Estádio do Dragão. A spectacular ride to experience is Line D (from Trindade, Aliados or São Bento), which crosses the river to Vila Nova de Gaia along the top tier of Ponte de Dom Luís I. Note that there is a major metro extension in progress west from São Bento to the Hospital Santo António, which will pass under much of the historic centre and cause potential disruption until 2022.

Buses and trams

Buses and **trams** are also run by STCP (see above). Major city bus stops include Praça Almeida Garrett opposite São Bento station, Praça da Liberdade at the bottom of Avenida dos Aliados, Jardim da Cordoaria and the interchange at Casa da Música metro station. On board, tickets cost €1.90, but it is cheaper if you have an Andante card (see box, p.124).

Porto's trams (*eléctricos*) run 5km

Useful bus routes

#500 from São Bento to the coast at Matosinhos via Ribeira, the Museu Vinho do Porto and Foz do Douro.

#502 from Bolhão to Matosinhos via Cedofeita, Boavista, Estádio de Bessa and Castelo do Queijo.

#207 from Campanha station to the Fundaçao de Serralves via the bus station, Aliados, Jardim do Palácio de Cristal and the Pousada de Juventude (youth hostel).

#208 from Aliados to Casa da Música and Boavista via Jardim do Palácio de Cristal.

#303 A circular route to and from Batalha via São Bento station, Torre dos Clérigos, Jardim da Cordoaria, Museu Nacional Soares dos Reis, Jardim do Palácio de Cristal, Casa da Música and Boavista..

Travel cards and tourist passes

To use the metro – and to save money on other forms of public transport – you need a rechargeable **Andante card**, which costs €0.60 and is available from ticket machines and from other marked Andante shops and kiosks (Lojas Andante). You credit the card with one, two or ten trips – the whole region is divided into concentric colour-coded zones, though everywhere you're going to want to go in Porto all falls within the same central zone 2. A single trip in the central zone costs €1.20 – you can change transport for free within the hour. It sounds complicated, but in practice it isn't, and you can change the instructions on the machines in every station to English.

If you're doing a lot of travelling, buy an **Andante Tour pass** (€7 for 24hr, €15 for 72hr), which is valid on all metros, buses and local trains. The pass is available on arrival at the airport from the Tourism Office in the Arrivals Hall.

If you are planning some intensive sight-seeing, the *turismos* also sell the **Porto Card** (€13 one day; €20 two days; €25 three days), which gives unlimited bus, metro and funicular travel plus discounts or free entry at many museums and monuments, wine cellars, bars, restaurants and shops. There are also streamlined versions (with no transport included) for €6, €10 or €13.

from Ribeira along the river to Foz do Douro (25min), with a branch from the Igreja do Carmo at Cordoaria in the city centre (using this, change halfway at Massarelos, by the tram museum). The service operates daily (9.15am–7pm; departures every 30min). Pay a flat €3 fare or get a 48hr ticket for €10.

Funicular

The quickest way from the city centre down to Ponte de Dom Luís I (for Vila Nova de Gaia) and Ribeira is via the **Funicular** (or *elevador*) **dos Guindais** (every 10min: May–June & Sept–Oct Mon–Wed & Sun 8am–10pm, Thurs–Sat 8am–midnight; Aug daily 8am–midnight; Nov–April daily 8am–8pm). Tickets cost €2.50 each way, or you can use the Andante card (see box, above).

Taxis

The minimum **taxi** fare is €3.25, with extra charged for luggage in the boot. A typical taxi ride across town costs €6–8, and most squares and major stations have taxi ranks (or call Radio Táxis T 225 073 900).

By bike

Porto's extremely hilly, and often cobbled, terrain might make **cycling** seem a no-no, but the Douro riverside actually makes a fine cycle way on both the north and south banks, with the most obvious routes being those that head out to the sea at Foz do Douro (or Afurada on the south side of the river). Bike hire is available from Biclas 7 Triclas near the north riverside at Rua da Arménia 30 (T 933 658 008, W https://tricia.pt; daily 9am–8pm) for €10 a day.

Road train

A **road train** trundles from the Sé to Vila Nova da Gaia (May–Sept roughly every 30min 9.30am–6pm, Oct–April hourly 10am–5pm; T 220 139 570, W magictrain.pt; the €10 fare includes a tasting at a port lodge).

Directory A–Z

Addresses
Addresses are written in the form "Rua do Crucifixo 50–4°", meaning the fourth storey of no. 50, Rua do Crucifixo. The addition of e, d or r/c at the end means the entrance is on the left (*esquerda*), right (*direita*) or on the ground floor (*rés-do-chão*).

Cinema
Mainstream films are shown at various multiplexes around the city, usually with Portuguese subtitles, and tickets are usually around €6. Listings can be found on filmspot.pt. One of the most central options is the wonderful Art Deco Cinema Trindade on Rua do Almada 412 (223 162 425, cinematrindade.pt).

Crime
For English-speaking police assistance go to the Esquadra de Turismo (Tourism Police Department), a branch of the PSP, at Rua Clube dos Fenianos 11, next to the main *turismo* (daily 8am–2am; 222 081 833). Violent crime is very rare but pickpocketing is common, especially on public transport.

Electricity
Portugal uses two-pin plugs (220–240v). UK appliances will work with a continental adaptor.

Health
Pharmacies, the first point of call if you are ill, are usually open Monday to Friday 9am–1pm & 3–7pm, Saturday 9am–1pm. One of the most central options, Farmácia Parente on Rua das Flores 116, is also open on Saturday afternoon.

Late-night and 24hr pharmacies (*farmácias de serviço*) operate on a rota basis; details are posted in the windows and given in the daily *Jornal de Notícias*, or call 118.

Hospital Santo António, Porto's main hospital, is located on Largo Prof Abel Salazar, near the university (222 077 500, chporto.pt).

Emergencies
For police, fire and ambulance services, dial 112.

Internet
Wi-fi is available, usually for free, in most cafés, restaurants and public spaces. You can also usually use computers in libraries, hotels and hostels, also usually without charge.

Left luggage
There are coin-operated lockers at Campanhã and São Bento train stations from around €4 a day for small bags, €7 for large ones.

LGBT travellers
For listings, support and news, visit portugalgay.pt (in Portuguese only).

Libraries
The Biblioteca Municipal Almeida Garrett at Palácio de Cristal, Rua Dom Manuel II (226 081 000) and the Biblioteca Municipal do Porto on Rua Dom João VI (225 193 480) are both open Monday and Saturday 10am–6pm, Tuesday to Friday 9am–7.30pm, except July and August Monday to Friday 10am–6pm.

Lost property
Try the Tourism Police Department, Rua Clube dos Fenianos 11, next to the main turismo (daily 8am–2am; 222 081 833).

Money
Portugal uses the euro (€). Banks open Monday to Friday 8.30am–3pm. Most central branches have automatic exchange machines for various currencies. You can withdraw up to €200 per day from ATMs ("Multibanco") – check fees with your home bank.

Opening hours

Most shops open Monday to Saturday 9am–7pm; smaller shops close for lunch (around 1–3pm) and on Saturday afternoons; shopping centres are open daily until 10pm or later. Most museums and monuments open Tuesday to Sunday from around 10am–6pm.

Post offices

Post offices (*correios*) are usually open Monday to Friday 8.30am–6pm. The main post office is on Praça General Humberto Delgado, by the town hall (Mon–Fri 8am–9pm, Sat 9am–6pm). Stamps (*selos*) are sold anywhere with the sign "Correio de Portugal – Selos".

Smoking

In common with the majority of other EU countries, smoking is prohibited in most restaurants and cafés.

Sports

Porto have punched above their weight in European football for many years. They have won the Portuguese league nearly thirty times, though their crowning glory was the European Cup win in 1987 and, the Champions League win in 2004 (they also won the UEFA Cup in 2003 and the Europa League in 2011). You can take a tour of Estádio do Dragão or buy match tickets (see p.43). You can also see top league action at the Estádio do Bessa, home to the city's second team, Boavista (see box, p.86).

Tickets

Tickets for most shows (usually in the range €10–40) can be bought in advance from the FNAC books and music store (see p.44), which also promotes gigs, events and talks. Porto's daily newspaper, the *Jornal de Notícias* is also a useful source of information.

Time

Portuguese time is the same as GMT. Clocks go forward an hour in late March and back to GMT in late October.

Tipping

Service charges are included in hotel and restaurant bills. A ten-percent tip is usual for restaurants; hotel porters and toilet attendants expect at least €0.50.

Toilets

There are very few public toilets, although most tourist sights have them (signed as *casa de banho, retrete, banheiro, lavabos* or "WC"). Gents are usually marked "H" (*homens*) or "C" (*cabalheiros*), and ladies "M" (*mulheres*) or "S" (*senhoras*).

Tourist information

The city's main tourist office is **Turismo Central,** Rua Clube dos Fenianos 25, top of Av dos Aliados (daily: May–July & Sept–Oct 9am–8pm; Aug 9am–9pm; Nov–April 9am–7pm; Ⓣ223 393 472), while the **Turismo Sé** is in the Casa da Câmara, Terreiro da Sé, opposite the cathedral (daily: May–Oct 9am–8pm; Nov–April 9am–7pm; Ⓣ223 393 472). There are also small information points on Praça da Liberdade (May–Oct daily 9.30am–6.30pm, Nov–April Mon–Fri 9.30am–5pm; Ⓣ223 393 472); in Campanhã train station (July–Aug only 9.30am–6.30pm,) and on the Ribeira waterfront at Praça da Ribeira (April–Oct daily 10.30am–7pm).

Vila Nova de Gaia has its own useful *turismo* on the waterfront at Av Diogo Leite 135 (April–Sept daily 10am–6pm; Oct–March Mon–Sat 10am–6pm; Ⓣ223 758 288, Ⓦcm-gaia.pt), which is geared almost exclusively to pointing you towards the port wine lodges.

There are also tourist offices at the day-trip destinations of: **Vila do Conde** at Rua 25 de Abril 103 (June to mid-Sept Mon–Fri 9am–7pm, Sat & Sun 9.30am–1pm & 2.30–6pm; mid-Sept to May Mon–Fri 9.30am–12.30 & 2–6pm; Ⓣ252 248 473, Ⓦwww.cm-viladoconde.pt); and **Amarante** at the Information Turismo, Largo Conselheiero António Candido (daily: June–Sept 9.30am–7pm;

Oct–May 9.30am–12.30pm & 2–6pm; 255 420 246, amarante.pt/turismo).

There are lots of **online information resources**, including the main tourist office website visitporto.travel which has detailed information in English on everything from the main sites to events, while there's more information about Porto and the north of Portugal on visitportoandnorth.travel. For a different view of the city, check out oportocool.wordpress.com, a blog of the city's fashionable hotspots (blog is in Portuguese).

Travellers with disabilities

Buses, metros and trains have access for people with disabilities (though not the trams). Public buildings are obliged to have disabled access, though be aware that many of Porto's streets are very steep and often cobbled. The Portuguese company SIA (sia.cm-porto.pt) has a map of accessible routes and buildings, while disabledholidays.com can arrange specialist holidays staying at hotels with disabled access. The main Portuguese tourism office also has a section on disabled travel on visitportugal.com/en/experiencias/turismo-acessivel.

Travelling with children

Portugal is very child-friendly and children are welcomed pretty much anywhere. Supermarkets sell nappies and pharmacies sell baby food and formula milk. However, Porto's steep and often cobbled streets aren't ideal for pushchairs and the sun can be strong.

Tours and cruises

Porto's stock-in-trade is the **river cruise** along the Douro. Services leave daily from the jetty at Ribeira, or opposite in Vila Nova da Gaia: they are frequent in the summer and reduced between November and February. The cheapest is the fifty-minute bridges cruise (€10), though there are also evening and dinner cruises, and full-day or weekend cruises, with prices ranging from €55 to €200. The longer cruises operate via the port wine town of Peso da Régua, halfway along the Douro, where you're either shuttled around a port wine lodge or go on a steam train.

There are a number of ways to explore Porto: **open-top bus tours** such as the Hop-On-Hop-Off tour (city-sightseeing.com) departing from Torre dos Clérigos from €14; **tuk-tuk tours** (tuktourporto.com) leaving from Rua de São Filipe de Nery from €20 per person for one hour; free three-hour-thirty-minute **walking tours** (http://portofreewalkingtour.wixsite.com/portofreewalkingtour/fashion) departing from Praça de Gomes Teixeira near the Livraria Lello bookshop; three-hour **bike tours** (from €15) departing from Avenida Aliados and three-hour **segway tours** (from €50) departing from Ribeira with Bluedragon City Tours (bluedragon.pt); and even **helicopter tours** from €150 (portoandlisbon.pt). Or try out a **Taste Porto Food Tour** (tasteporto.com), which focuses on local gastronomy (3hr 30min tours from €62). **Porto Tours** at Rua Clube dos Fenianos 25 (daily 10am–7pm; 222 000 045, portotours.com), can book all kinds of tours, including river cruises, classic car tours and Vespa tours. **Cooltour Oporto** (Rua Júlio Dinis 728- 3; 222 010 213, cooltouroporto.com) offers package trips and personalized trips around Porto, and further afield for example in the Minho region.

Festivals and events

You can check exact festival and event dates on Porto's tourism website Ⓦportoturismo.pt and on Ⓦvisitportugal.com/en. One-off and less mainstream events can be found on Ⓦinfoporto.pt, which has information in both Portuguese and English. Ⓦviralagenda.com/pt/porto is another good resource but is only in Portuguese.

Fantasporto

February–March Ⓦfantasporto.com. The respected international fantasy, sci-fi and thriller film festival, has been a fixture in the city since 1980. The festival runs over ten days and takes place at the Rivoli Theatre, at Rua do Bonjardim 143.

Queima das Fitas do Porto

May

The city's "burning of the ribbons" represents the big end-of-year festival for Porto's students (the ribbons representing the various faculties). There are concerts and fado performances throughout the city, as well as a procession in the Parque da Cidade.

São João

June

Porto lets its hair down during the exuberant celebration that is the Festa de São João, St John's Eve (the night of June 23–24), in honour of John the Baptist, patron saint of the city. Be warned, for one night only it is considered fair game to bash total strangers over the head, traditionally with leeks, though now these have been replaced by even more irritating squeaky plastic hammers. There are free concerts throughout the night and a massive firework display at midnight over the river at Praça da Ribeira. The following morning there's a traditional Rabelo boat regatta on the Douro.

Festas da Cidade

June

The Festa de São João party is the highlight of the wider city festival, the Festas da Cidade, that runs throughout June and celebrates the start of the summer with concerts, dances, vintage car rallies, regattas, sardine grills and other entertainments – like the competitive cascata displays (dolls depicting Santo António, São João and São Pedro, complete with miniature houses, trains and cars).

Festa da Cerveja

June

The annual Festa da Cerveja (Beer Fest) runs for five days in the Jardim do Palácio de Cristal, with around 200 national and international craft beers together with street-food stalls and live music.

Public holidays

In addition to Christmas (Dec 24–25) and New Year's Day (Jan 1), public holidays include Good Friday (March/April); April 25 (Liberty Day); May 1 (Labour Day); June 10 (Portugal/Camões Day); June 24 (São João, Porto only); August 15 (Feast of the Assumption); 5 October (Republic Day); 1 November (All Saints' Day); December 1 (Independence Day); December 8 (Immaculate Conception) .

Nos Primavera Sound

June

nosprimaverasound.com. A big music festival in the Parque da Cidade. The 2017 line-up included Bon Iver, Aphex Twin, Justice and Teenage Fanclub.

Fazer a Festa International Theatre Festival

July teatroartimagem.org. This major international theatre festival has 30 professional theatre companies and around 60 theatrical performances held in squares, gardens and cultural spaces around the city, aimed particularly at getting young people into theatre.

LGBT Porto Pride

July

First held in 2001 and growing in size each year, the annual LGBT Porto Pride march and celebration takes place in the first or second week of July, departing from Praça da República.

The Porto Wine Fest

July

Taking place along the river front at Vila Nova de Gaia, the Porto Wine Fest features tastings, food stalls showcasing leading chefs and events laid on by the major port-wine lodges.

Noites Ritual

September

The Noites Ritual is an exclusively Portuguese music festival with performances at the Rota Mota Pavilion in the Jardim do Palácio de Cristal. Free entry.

Porto Jazz Festival

September portajazz.com

Porto's jazz festival is held during the month in the Jardim do Palácio de Cristal, with local and international performers.

Red Bull Air Races

September airrace.redbull.com.

Not for the faint hearted, these air races see pilots doing dare-devil flying along the narrow Douro river valley along a course marked by giant "air-gate" cones. The start and finish are at the Douro estuary by Foz do Douro.

Christmas

December

The Christmas period in Porto sees the historic centre decked in Christmas lights. The main celebration is Midnight Mass on 24 December followed by a meal of *bacalhau*. Some cafés and restaurants are open on 25 December.

Corrida de São Silvestre and New Year

December

A running race departing from Av dos Aliados to mark the end of the year. New Year is welcomed with a firework display over the river, after which you can find traditional *bolo rei* cakes in cafés and shops.

Chronology

4th century AD Romans form a port on the north bank of the Douro and call it Portus Cale.

711–868 Moorish occupation, which ends when a Christian warlord, Count Vimara Peres, takes control of the district between the Minho and the Douro, which is now called Condado de Portucale.

1095 Henri of Burgundy is granted the land around Portucale. His son, Afonso Henriques, becomes king of a newly independent country named Portugal.

1111 Bishop Hugo begins work on the city's cathedral and walls as the city grows around the Ribeira.

12th century The beginning of port-wine production. Grapes are taken to the lodges on the humid south side of the river in Vila Nova de Gaia where conditions are best, and Porto begins to export port.

1387 After staying in the church of São Francisco, Dom João I marries Philippa of Lancaster in Porto to cement the alliance between England and Portugal. The city begins to grow.

1394 The son of Philippa of Lancaster and João I, Henry the Navigator, is born in Porto. He becomes the driving force behind Portugal's explorations of the oceans. Sturdy city walls are built to protect Porto from attack.

15th–17th century Porto becomes one of the largest shipbuilding centres in the country as Portugal's navigators expand the country's maritime empire, which extends from Brazil in the west to Macau in the east.

1415 Porto residents donate meat to sailors heading off to conquer Ceuta in Africa, keeping only tripe to feed themselves. From this time on, Porto residents are known as *tripeiros*, and it is still a local speciality.

16th century AD Under Dom Manuel I, the riverside city expands outwards, with the creation of streets such as Rua das Flores and churches such as the Convento de Santa Clara and Mosteiro de São Bento da Vitoria.

1703 The Methuen Treaty between Portugal and England stimulates trade with Britain and guarantees sales of port at a time when standard wines were hard to come by in England because of war with the French.

1717 The first English factory is set up in Porto as the port industry becomes run largely by the British.

1757 The Marquês de Pombal creates the Demarcated Region of the Alto Douro to control the quality of wine production.

17th–18th century AD Public works projects see the building of the Torre de Clérigos. The millinery industry grows up as the city becomes more industrialized, with textiles, ironmongery and linen the other mainstays. Most of the city walls are demolished to make way for development.

1809 Napoleon occupies Porto. Many residents die when fleeing across a flimsy pontoon bridge over the Douro. Napoleon is soon driven from city, with the help of the British who, under Wellington, cross the Douro on port boats to chase out the French.

1832–1834 Liberal Porto residents resist an 18-month siege by the anti-liberal constitution troops loyal to Dom Miguel during the Portuguese civil war, establishing the Porto residents' reputation for being tough.

19th century Industrialization continues, with many ceramics factories opening. The century also sees the building of the Mercado do Bolhão, the laying out of city parks, the arrival of gas street lighting and water supplies.

1843 The first permanent bridge is built over the Douro, the Ponte Pênsil, which is soon replaced in 1886 by the Ponte de Dom Luís I, built by Teophile Seyrig, a partner of Eiffel.

1877 The Ponte Maria Pia opens for Porto's railway, built by Gustave Eiffel. It is replaced by the Ponte de São João in 1991.

1890 Economic recession leads to a republican revolt in Porto which eventually leads to the creation of the Portuguese Republic in 1910.

1915 The main square, Aliados, is laid out to form a northern border to the old centre.

1919 A counter-revolution in Porto to re-establish the monarchy is quickly put down.

1933 The Instituto dos Vinhos do Douro e do Porto is set up to regulate the port wine trade.

1945 Porto's airport opens 11km north west of the centre.

1950s Sales of port slump after World War II. Many independent port companies are bought out by international drinks chains.

1970s Taylors launch Late Bottled Vintage Port, a quality port which was more affordable than vintage.

1996 Porto is named a UNESCO World Heritage Site.

2001 Porto is named European Capital of Culture.

2002 The first metro line opens in Porto. It extends to the airport in 2006.

2004 The Estádio do Dragão is built to host the football European Championships, in the same year as José Mourinho's FC Porto win the Europeam Champions League.

2009 Ryanair become the first low-cost airline to fly to Porto. Others soon follow suit as Porto becomes a popular city-break destination.

2015 A new cruise terminal opens at Leixões, north of the city.

2017 Plans to extend the metro west from São Bento are announced.

Language

English is widely spoken in most of Porto's hotels and tourist restaurants, but you will find a few words of Portuguese extremely useful. Written Portuguese is similar to Spanish, though pronunciation is very different. Vowels are often nasal or ignored altogether. The consonant, at least, are consistent:

Consonants

c is soft before e and i, hard otherwise unless it has a cedilla – *açúcar* (sugar) is pronounced "assookar".

ch is somewhat softer than in English; *chá* (tea) sounds like Shah.

j is like the "s" in pleasure, as is g except when it comes before a "hard" vowel (a, o and u).

lh sounds like "lyuh".

q is always pronounced as a "k".

s before a consonant or at the end of a word becomes "sh", otherwise it's as in English – *caracóis* (snails) is pronounced "Karakoish".

x is also pronounced "sh"– Baixa is pronounced "Baisha".

Vowels

e/é e at the end of a word is silent unless it has an accent, so that *carne* (meat) is pronounced "karn", while *café* is "caf-ay".

ã or õ the tilde renders the pronunciation much like the French -an and -on endings, only more nasal.

ão this sounds something like a strangled "Ow!" cut off in midstream (as in *pão*, bread – *são*, saint – *limão*, lemon).

ei this sounds like "ay" (as in *feito* – finished).

ou this sounds like "oh" (as in *roupa* – clothes).

Words and phrases

Basics

yes	sim
no	não
hello	olá
good morning	bom dia
good afternoon/night	boa tarde/noite
goodbye	adeus
see you later	até logo
today	hoje
tomorrow	amanhã
please	por favor/se faz favor
everything all right?	tudo bem?
it's all right/OK	está bem
thank you (male / female speaker)	obrigado/a
where	onde
what	que
when	quando
why	porquê
how	como
how much	quanto
I don't know	não sei
do you know...?	sabe...?
could you...?	pode...?
is there...? there is	há...? (silent "h")
do you have...? (pron. "taying")	tem...?
I'd like...	queria...
sorry	desculpe
excuse me	com licença
do you speak English?	fala Inglês?
I don't understand	não compreendo
this	este/a
that	esse/a
now	agora
later	mais tarde
more	mais
less	menos
big	grande
little	pequeno
open	aberto
closed	fechado
women	senhoras
men	homens
toilet/bathroom	lavabo/quarto de banho

Getting around

left	esquerda
right	direita
straight ahead	sempre em frente
here	aqui
there	ali
near	perto

far	longe
Where is ...	Onde é...
the bus station?	a estação de camionetas?
the bus stop for...	a paragem de autocarro para...
Where does the bus to...leave from?	Donde parte o autocarro para...?
What time does it leave? (arrive at...?)	A que horas parte (chega a...?) ?
Stop here please	Pare aqui por favor
ticket (to)	bilhete (para)
return trip	ida e volta

Common signs

open	aberto
closed	fechado
entrance	entrada
exit	saída
pull	puxe
push	empurre
lift	elevador
pay in advance	pré-pagamento
danger/ous	perigo/perigoso
no parking	proibido estacionar
(road) works	obras

Accommodation

I'd like a room	Queria um quarto
It's for one night (week)	É para uma noite (semana)
It's for one person (two people)	É para uma pessoa (duas pessoas)
How much is it?	Quanto custa?
May I see/ look?	Posso ver?
Is there a cheaper room?	Há um quarto mais barato?
with a shower	com duche

Shopping

How much is it?	Quanto é?
bank; change	banco; câmbio
post office	correios
(two) stamps	(dois) selos
What's this called in Portuguese?	Como se diz isto em Português?
What's that?	O que é isso?
sale	saldo
sold out	esgotado

Days of the week

Sunday	Domingo
Monday	Segunda-feira
Tuesday	Terça-feira
Wednesday	Quarta-feira
Thursday	Quinta-feira
Friday	Sexta-feira
Saturday	Sábado

Months

January	Janeiro
February	Fevereiro
March	Março
April	Abril
May	Maio
June	Junho
July	Julho
August	Agosto
September	Setembro
October	Outubro
November	Novembro
December	Dezembro

Useful words

glazed, painted tile	azulejo
quay	cais
chapel	capela
house	casa
shopping centre	centro commercial
station	estação
street/road	estrada/rua
fair or market	feira
church	igreja
garden	jardim
viewpoint/belvedere	miradouro
square	praça/largo

Numbers

1	um/uma
2	dois/duas
3	três
4	quatro
5	cinco
6	seis
7	sete
8	oito
9	nove
10	dez
11	onze

12	doze
13	treze
14	catorze
15	quinze
16	dezasseis
17	dezassete
18	dezoito
19	dezanove
20	vinte
21	vinte e um
30	trinta
40	quarenta
50	cinquenta
60	sessenta
70	setenta
80	oitenta
90	noventa
100	cem
101	cento e um
200	duzentos
500	quinhentos
1000	mil

Food and drink

Basics

assado	roasted
colher	spoon
conta	bill
copo	glass
cozido	boiled
ementa	menu
estrelado/frito	fried
faca	knife
garfo	fork
garrafa	bottle
grelhado	grilled
mexido	scrambled

Menu terms

almoço	lunch
ementa turística	set menu
entradas	starters
especialidades	speciality
jantar	dinner
lista de vinhos	wine list
pequeno almoço	breakfast
petiscos	tapas-like snacks
prato do dia	dish of the day
sobremesa	dessert

Soups, salad and staples

açucár	sugar
arroz	rice
azeitonas	olives
batatas fritas	chips/french fries
caldo verde	cabbage soup
fruta	fruit
legumes	vegetables
manteiga	butter
massa	pasta
molho (de tomate /piri-piri)	tomato/chilli sauce)
omeleta	omelette
ovos	eggs
pão	bread
pimenta	pepper
piri-piri	chilli sauce
queijo	cheese
sal	salt
salada	salad
sopa de legumes	vegetable soup
sopa de marisco	shellfish soup
sopa de peixe	fish soup

Fish and shellfish

atum	tuna
camarões	shrimp
carapau	mackerel
cherne	stone bass
dourada	bream
espada	scabbard fish
espadarte	swordfish
gambas	prawns
lagosta	lobster
lulas (grelhadas)	squid (grilled)
mexilhões	mussels
pescada	hake
polvo	octopus
robalo	sea bass
salmão	salmon
salmonete	red mullet
santola	spider crab
sapateira	crab
sardinhas	sardines
tamboril	monkfish
truta	trout
viera	scallop

Meat

alheira	chicken sausage
borrego	lamb
chanfana	lamb or goat casserole
chouriço	spicy sausage
coelho	rabbit
cordeiro	lamb
dobrada/tripa	tripe
espetada mista	mixed meat kebab
febras	pork steaks
fiambre	ham
fígado	liver
frango na brasa	chicken grilled over hot coals
frango no churrasco	barbecued chicken
leitão	roast suckling pig
pato	duck
perdiz	partridge
perú	turkey
picanha	strips of beef in garlic sauce
presunto	smoked ham
rim	kidney
rodizio	barbecued meats
rojões	cubed pork cooked in blood with potatoes
vitela	veal

Portuguese specialities

açorda	bread-based stew (often seafood)
arroz de marisco	seafood rice
bife à portuguesa	thin beef steak with a fried egg on top
bacalhau à brás	salted cod with egg and potatoes
bacalhau na brasa	salted cod roasted with potatoes
bacalhau à Gomes de Sá	salted cod baked with potatoes, egg and olives
caldeirada	fish stew
cataplana	fish, shellfish or meat stewed in a circular metal dish
cozido à portuguesa	boiled casserole of meat and beans, served with rice and vegetables
feijoada	bean stew with meat and vegetables
filletes de pescada	hake fillets in a light batter
francesinha	toasted meat sandwich with cheese sauce
migas	meat or fish in a bready garlic sauce
pataniscas	*bacalhau* patties, salted cod cakes
porco à alentejana	pork cooked with clams
tripas à modo do Porto	tripe and bean stew

Snacks and desserts

arroz doce	rice pudding
bifana	steak sandwich
bolo	cake
gelado	ice cream
pastéis de bacalhau	salted cod and potato cakes
pastel de nata	custard tart
prego	steak sandwich
pudim	crème caramel
tosta	toasted sandwich

Drinks

água (sem/com gás)	mineral water (without/with gas)
café	coffee
cerveja	beer
chá	tea
fresca/natural	chilled/room temperature
sem/com leite	without/with milk
sem/com açúcar	without/with sugar
sumo de laranja/maçã	orange/apple juice
um copo/uma garrafa de/da...	a glass/bottle of...
vinho branco/tinto	white/red wine

Publishing information

This 1st edition published February 2018 by **Rough Guides Ltd**
80 Strand, London WC2R 0RL
11, Community Centre, Panchsheel Park, New Delhi 110017, India
Distributed by Penguin Random House
Penguin Books Ltd, 80 Strand, London WC2R 0RL
Penguin Group (USA) 345 Hudson Street, NY 10014, USA
Penguin Group (Australia) 250 Camberwell Road, Camberwell, Victoria 3124, Australia
Penguin Group (NZ) 67 Apollo Drive, Mairangi Bay, Auckland 1310, New Zealand
Penguin Group (South Africa) Block D, Rosebank Office Park, 181 Jan Smuts Avenue, Parktown North, Gauteng, South Africa 2193
Rough Guides is represented in Canada by
DK Canada 320 Front Street West, Suite 1400, Toronto, Ontario M5V 3B6
Typeset in Minion and Din to an original design by Henry Iles and Dan May.
Printed and bound in China

144pp includes index
A catalogue record for this book is available from the British Library
ISBN 978-0-24131-845-4

1 3 5 7 9 8 6 4 2

Rough Guides credits

Editor: Olivia Rawes
Layout: Ankur Guha
Cartography: Ed Wright
Picture editor: Aude Vauconsant
Photographer: XX
Proofreader: Jennifer Speake
Managing editor: Keith Drew
Production: Jimmy Lao
Cover photo research: XXX
Editorial assistant: Aimee White
Senior DTP coordinator: Dan May
Publishing director: Georgina Dee

The authors

Matthew Hancock has lived and worked in Portugal and has explored nearly every corner of the country as co-author of the Rough Guide to Portugal. He is also author of the Rough Guide to Lisbon. Now a writer and editor based in Dorset, he is also co-author of the Rough Guide to Hampshire, Dorset and the Isle of Wight.

Amanda Tomlin has worked as a Rough Guide editor for twenty-five years. She has lived in and travelled widely throughout Portugal and has contributed to the Rough Guides to Lisbon and Portugal. She is also co-author of Rough Guide to Hampshire, Dorset and the Isle of Wight.

Acknowledgements

Matthew Hancock & Amanda Tomlin Many thanks to everyone who helped with this first edition, especially Raquel Rodrigues at the Porto Convention and Visitors Bureau, Olga and Fernando at Inpatio, Miguel at Flattered, Susana at the 1872 River House, Amy O'Rourke and The Yeatman, everyone at Flores Village, António Padeira and Alexandra and Brent Weld. Special thanks to Alex and Olivia for their usual support, and making research trips such fun. Thanks too for the excellent editing and support of Olivia Rawes, Ed Wright and Keith Drew at Rough Guides.

Help us update

We've gone to a lot of effort to ensure that the first edition of the **Pocket Rough Guide Porto** is accurate and up-to-date. However, things change – places get "discovered", opening hours are notoriously fickle, restaurants and rooms raise prices or lower standards. If you feel we've got it wrong or left something out, we'd like to know, and if you can remember the address, the price, the hours, the phone number, so much the better.

Please send your comments with the subject line "**Pocket Rough Guide Porto Update**" to mail@roughguides.com. We'll credit all contributions and send a copy of the next edition (or any other Rough Guide if you prefer) for the very best emails.

Photo credits

All photos © Rough Guides except the following:
(Key: t-top; c-centre; b-bottom; l-left; r-right)

Cover: Porto skyline from across the Douro River **Alamy Stock Photo:** Sean Pavone

1 Alamy Stock Photo: Hercules Milas
2 Alamy Stock Photo: CW Images (tl); Jeremy Pembrey (br). **AWL Images:** Hemis (bl). Robert Harding Picture Library: James Strachan (tr)
4 Getty Images: Raquel Maria Carbonell Pagola
5 4Corners: Hans-Georg Eiben
10 Alamy Stock Photo: Sean Pavone
11 AWL Images: Mauricio Abreu (tl); ImageBroker (cr); Nick Ledger (br)
12 Getty Images: John Harper (t). **Rua Tapas & Music Bar:** Renato ribeiro (b)
13 4Corners: Hans-Georg Eiben (b). AWL Images: Nick Ledger (t)
14 Alamy Stock Photo: Anthony Palmer (t). **Robert Harding Picture Library:** Arco Images / Therin-Weise (b)
15 4Corners: Claudio Cassaro (c). **Alamy Stock Photo:** Cal Sport Media (t); Travel Pix (b)
16 4Corners: Guido Cozzi (b). **AWL Images:** Nick Ledger (t)
17 Robert Harding Picture Library: Guy Thouvenin (t)
18 Dreamstime.com: Joyfull (b); Zts (t); TasFoto (c)
19 Dreamstime.com: Coplandj (t). **Getty Images:** Universal Images Group Editorial (b). **iStockphoto.com:** fxegs (c)
20 Alamy Stock Photo: Raj Singh (t); Tim E White (c). Dreamstime.com: Diana Carapuço (b)
21 Alamy Stock Photo: Hercules Milas (c); Paul Street (t). Rex Shutterstock: Shutterstock / REX / Epa / Jose Coelho (b)

22 Alamy Stock Photo: Michael Brooks (c). **Dreamstime.com:** Lukasz Janyst (b); TasFoto (t)
23 Alamy Stock Photo: Hemis (t); Hemis (c). **Rex Shutterstock:** Shutterstock / REX / Epa / Jose Coelho (b)
24-25 AWL Images: Nick Ledger
26 AWL Images: Hemis
27 123RF.com: perszing1982
30 Getty Images: National Geographic Magazines
31 Getty Images: Blend Images
32 Portosigns
34 O Comercial: Pedro Mendes
35 The Wine Box: Gonçalo
37 4Corners: Claudio Cassaro
40 Alamy Stock Photo: Manfred Gottschalk
42 AWL Images: Hemis
44 Alamy Stock Photo: Paul Quayle
45 Alamy Stock Photo: Alex Segre
47 Guindalense futebal clube
50 iStockphoto.com: Getty Images / efired
53 AWL Images: Alan Copson
54 Alamy Stock Photo: Jackietraveller Porto
55 Alamy Stock Photo: Karol Kozlowski Premium RM Collection
56 Alamy Stock Photo: M Sobreira
57 Porto Convention & Visitors Bureau
58 iStockphoto.com: ptxgarfield
59 Plano B
60 AWL Images: Michele Falzone
64 Alamy Stock Photo: age fotostock
66 Porto Convention & Visitors Bureau
68 3maisarte: Miguel Marques
69 Alamy Stock Photo: Danita Delimont
70 AWL Images: M Sobreira
71 The Yeatman Hotel
72 Porto Convention & Visitors Bureau
73 Alamy Stock Photo: Hercules Milas
76 Dreamstime.com: Leonid Andronov
78 Alamy Stock Photo: Juanma Aparicio
79 scar-id store
80 Alamy Stock Photo: Tim E White
81 Alamy Stock Photo: Mark Dunn
82 Getty Images: Miguel Riopa
83 Alamy Stock Photo: blickwinkel
87 Dreamstime.com: José Carvalho
88 Gail Aguiar
89 daTerra
91 Getty Images: Moment Open / Helena Paixão
95 Rex Shutterstock: Shutterstock / REX / Epa / Jose Coelho
97 Getty Images: UIG via Getty Images
98 Porto Convention & Visitors Bureau
99 Alamy Stock Photo: kpzfoto
100 Dreamstime.com: Fotografiecor
103 Getty Images: Moment RF / Angel Gonzalez
104 Luc Hermans
105 Vila do Conde Municipal Arquive
106 Getty Images: Photononstop RM / Bruno Barbier
108 Alamy Stock Photo: Art Collection 4
110 Alamy Stock Photo: Paul Street
111 Hans Peter Bachofen
112-113 Alamy Stock Photo: Adventure Pictures / Marcin Jamkowski
120-121 iStockphoto.com: Getty Images / photooiasson

Index

Maps are marked in **bold**.

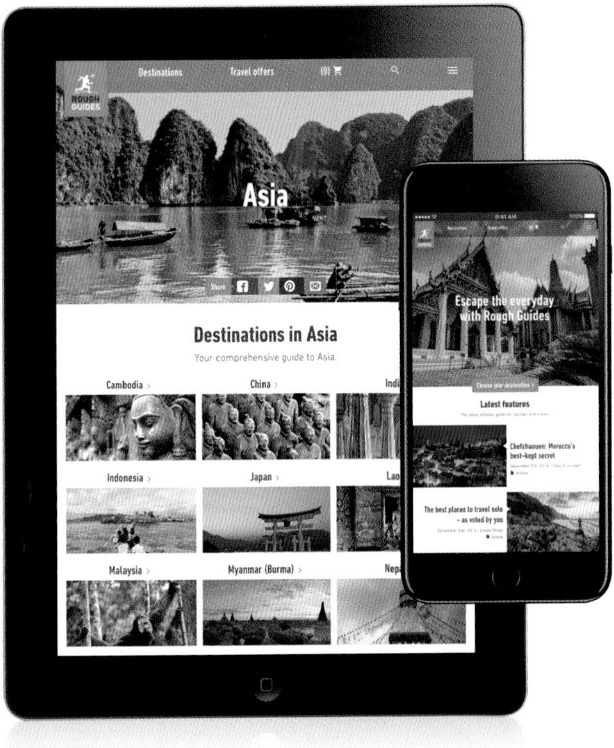

Long bus journey? Phone run out of juice?

TEST YOUR KNOWLEDGE WITH OUR ROUGH GUIDES TRAVEL QUIZ

1. **Denim, the pencil, the stethoscope and the hot-air balloon were all invented in which country?**
   a. Italy
   b. France
   c. Germany
   d. Switzerland

2. **What is the busiest airport in the world?**
   a. London Heathrow
   b. Tokyo International
   c. Chicago O'Hare
   d. Hartsfield-Jackson Atlanta International

3. **Which of these countries does not have the equator running through it?**
   a. Brazil
   b. Tanzania
   c. Indonesia
   d. Colombia

4. **What is the principal religion of Japan?**
   a. Confucianism
   b. Buddhism
   c. Jainism
   d. Shinto

5. **Every July in Sonkajärvi, central Finland, contestants gather for the World Championships of which sport?**
   a. Zorbing
   b. Wife-carrying
   c. Chess-boxing
   d. Extreme ironing

6. **What colour are post boxes in Germany?**
   a. Red
   b. Green
   c. Blue
   d. Yellow

7. **For three days each April during Songkran festival in Thailand, people take to the streets to throw what at each other?**
   a. Water
   b. Oranges
   c. Tomatoes
   d. Underwear

For more quizzes, competitions and inspirational features go to **roughguides.com**

1:b / 2:d / 3:b / 4:d / 5:b / 6:d / 7:a